Henry MacMahon

The Order Followed in the Consecration of a Bishop

According to the Roman Pontifical

Henry MacMahon

The Order Followed in the Consecration of a Bishop According to the Roman Pontifical

ISBN/EAN: 9783744653640

Printed in Europe, USA, Canada, Australia, Japan

Cover: Foto ©Lupo / pixelio.de

More available books at **www.hansebooks.com**

ORDO
Consecrationis Electi
IN
EPISCOPUM
JUXTA
PONTIFICALE ROMANUM

Cum Appendice
CURANTE
R. D. JOSEPHO HENRICO McMAHON
Moderatore Bibliothecæ Cathedralis Neo-Eboracensis

Impensis Bibliothecæ Cathedralis
Neo-Eboracensis, Madison Avenue, 460.
MDCCCXCVI.

THE ORDER FOLLOWED IN THE CONSECRATION OF A BISHOP,

ACCORDING TO THE

ROMAN PONTIFICAL.

With an Appendix.
Translated and Edited by
THE REV. JOSEPH HENRY McMAHON,
Director of the Cathedral Library of New York.

The Cathedral Library Association,
460 Madison Avenue, N. Y.
1896.

APPROBATIO.

Revisione rite peracta, hanc editionem novissimo exemplari typico Pontificalis Romani esse conformem testamur. In fidem, etc.

Neo-Eboraci ex aedibus Archiepiscopalibus hac die 30 Martii 1892.

Pro Illmo et Rev^{mo} MICHAELE AUGUSTINO, Archiepiscopo.

       Gherardus Ferrante,
           Substitutus.

Michael Augustinus Corrigan.

DEI ET APOSTOLICÆ SEDIS
GRATIA ARCHIEPISCOPUS NEO-EBORACENSIS, SS. DD. PRAELATUS DOMESTICUS, SOLIO PONTIFICIO ASSISTENS.

PUS quod inscribitur "Ordo Consecrationis Electi in Episcopum cum appendice," cura et expensis Bibliothecæ Cathedralis imprimi potest et evulgari.

Datum Neo-Eboraci, die 30 Martii 1892.

      ✠ Michael Augustinus,
        Archiepiscopus Neo-Ebor.

DECRETUM.

Quum Cæremoniarum Magister Ecclesiæ Cathedralis Neo Eboracensis Diœceseos in Statibus Fœderatis Americæ Septentrionalis de consensu Episcopi a Sacra Rituum Congregatione declarari petierit:

"Utrum pro majori Fidelium utilitate, qui linguam "latinam non callent, licitum sit addere versionem "in lingua vulgari textui latino Pontificalis Romani, "et præsertim illi parti, quæ Ordinum collationem "respicit. uti exhibetur in exemplari cui titulus.— "Ritus Ordinationum juxta Pontificale Romanum.— "Curante Rev. J. S. M. Lynch in Seminario Pro- "vinciali apud Trojam, N. Y. Sacræ Liturgiæ Pro- "fessore, etc., etc."

Sacra eadem Congregatio, referente subscripto Secretario ita rescripsit:—Detur Decretum in una Neo Eboracen., diei 4 Augusti 1877. Atque ita rescripsit die 3 Februarii 1879.

   D. CARDINALIS BARTOLINIUS, S. R. C.
               Præfectus.

PLAC. RALLI, *S. R. C. Secrius.*

DECREE.

When, with the consent of his Ordinary, the master of ceremonies at the Cathedral Church of the diocese of New York, United States of America, petitioned the Sacred Congregation of Rites to declare "whether for the greater benefit of the faithful who do not understand the Latin Text of the Roman Pontifical; in particular to that part which treats of the conferring of Orders, as has been done in a volume entitled "The Rite of Ordination," according to the Roman Pontifical, by Rev. J. S. M. Lynch, Professor of Sacred Liturgy in the Provincial Seminary, at Troy, N. Y., etc., etc. The Sacred Congregation, through the undersigned secretary answered, on Feb. 3d, 1879, as follows: Let the Decree of Aug. 4th, 1877, in a case proposed by New York, stand.

CARDINAL BARTOLINI,
Prefect.
MONS. PLACIDO RALLI, *Secretary of the S. C. R.*

Director quarumdam Ephemeridum Catholicarum, quæ typis cuduntur Neo Eboraci, a Sacra Rituum Congregatione declarari petiit num prohibitum sit in libris nuncupatis *Devotionis* textui latino Ordinis Missæ, ac præsertim Canonis, addere versionem in lingua vulgari? Sacra vero Rituum Congregatio, referente infrascripto Secretario, audito voto R. P. D. Laurentii Salvati S. Fidei Promotoris, declarare censuit: Libros eorumque versiones in lingua vernacula, de quibus agitur, a canonicis præscriptionibus et Apostolicis Decretis, Episcoporum auctoritati omnino reservari; ideoque licitum non esse Fidelibus horum uti editionibus, nisi istæ expressam præseferant Episcoporum adprobationem. Atque ita declaravit die 4 Augusti, 1877. (5703, Neo Eboracen.)

The director of a certain Catholic journal published in New York, petitioned the Sacred Congregation of Rites to declare if it were forbidden (in books of devotion) to add a translation in the vernacular to the Latin text of the Ordinary of the Mass, and particularly to the Canon. The Sacred Congregation of Rites, after hearing the opinion of the Rev. Lawrence Salvati, Promoter of the Faith, declared through the undersigned Secretary: "that books of the kind under consideration, and translations of them in the vernacular are entirely reserved, by the canonical regulations and Apostolic decrees, to the authority of the bishops; and that, therefore, it is unlawful for the faithful to use any edition of the same unless it bear the express approbation of the bishops." And so it was declared August 4th, 1877.

(5703, New York).

INTRODUCTION.

THE fact that five thousand copies of this little manual have been sold is an indication of the service it has rendered in enabling the laity to understand better the sublime function whose ceremonies it describes. The many letters of congratulation received upon this attempt to present in an attractive form this portion of the liturgy is at once a satisfaction and an incentive. The mere reading of the ceremonies and prayers will throw light upon the symbolical meaning where disquisitions would be dry and meaningless. It is not deemed necessary, therefore, to enlarge upon the ceremonies, further than to call attention to the principal divisions.

The function may properly be divided

INTRODUCTION.

into the preliminary examination, the consecration proper, and the investiture. The first part includes the form of ascertaining solemnly that the Bishop Elect has the right to Episcopal consecration; of receiving his oath of submission to the Holy See, the centre of unity; and of inquiring into the orthodoxy of his faith. The form of oath embodied in this manual is that prescribed for the Bishops of the United States in the Second Council of Baltimore. In the examination the Bishop Elect is made to profess categorically his belief in the different matters of faith that have been particularly attacked by heretics, especially the doctrine of the Incarnation. These preliminaries having been duly gone through with, the Mass is begun, its simultaneous celebration by Consecrator and Bishop Elect betokening the unity of their faith.

INTRODUCTION.

Immediately after the Gradual or Tract, the Consecration ceremony begins with the solemn announcement by the Consecrator of the awful duties of a Bishop. The different rites and prayers sufficiently indicate their purpose. The majesty of the plain chant in the Litanies, the Veni Creator, and the Preface is perhaps unsurpassed by any other portion of the liturgy.

The Consecration ceremony proper being finished, the new Bishop is invested with the crosier and ring proper to the Episcopal order, the prayers and admonitions accompanying the investiture clearly indicating their uses and purposes.

The Mass proceeds with the Consecrator and new Bishop celebrating in unison at the same altar. After the Communion (the new Bishop communicating both of the Sacred Host and Precious Blood) the new Bishop receives the mitre and gloves,

INTRODUCTION.

which have been solemnly blessed by the Consecrator. Then with the utmost pomp the new Bishop is enthroned on the Episcopal seat while the magnificent *Te Deum* is intoned. During the hymn he is led between the two assistant Bishops around the church, blessing the people as he goes. Afterward he is received by the Consecrator to the kiss of peace, and the function is ended.

Those only who appreciate the hierarchical importance of the Episcopate will thoroughly understand the sublimity of the whole ceremony.

Feast of St. John de Matha, 1894.

DE CONSECRATIONE ELECTI
IN EPISCOPUM.

NEMO consecrari debet, nisi prius constet Consecratori de commissione consecrandi, sive per litteras Apostolicas, si sit extra curiam, sive per commissionem vivæ vocis oraculo, a Summo Pontifice Consecratori factam, si Consecrator ipse sit Cardinalis.

Statuta die Consecrationis, quæ debet esse Dominica, vel Natalitium Apostolorum, vel etiam festiva, si Summus Pontifex hoc specialiter indulserit: et tam Consecrator, quam Electus conveniens est, ut præcedenti die jejunent.

Consecratio, si extra curiam Romanam fiat, in Ecclesia, ad quam promoti fuerint, aut in provincia, si commode fieri poterit, celebretur.

In Ecclesia, ubi fiet consecratio, ornantur duæ capellæ, major pro Consecrante, et minor pro Electo. Et in majori quidem, super altari parato, ut est moris, erit crux in medio, et ad minus quatuor candelabra. In terra ad gradus altaris erunt tapetia strata, super quibus procumbit Electus, sed Consecrator, et alii genuflectent.

Paratur etiam in loco propinquo et congruo credentia pro Consecratore, super quam erit mappa munda: duo candelabra; vasa ad abluendum manus,

THE CONSECRATION OF A BISHOP.

NO one is to be consecrated unless first the Consecrator shall be sure of the commission to consecrate, either by apostolic letters, if he be outside the *curia*, or by verbal commission given by the Sovereign Pontiff to the Consecrator, if the Consecrator himself be a cardinal. The day chosen for consecration should be a Sunday or the feast day of one of the apostles,* or it may be even a feast day if the Sovereign Pontiff shall have made this special concession; and it is fitting that both the Consecrator and the elect should fast on the preceding day. If the consecration be performed outside of the Roman *curia*, it should be held in the diocese to which the Bishop-elect has been promoted, or within the province, if it can be conveniently done. In the church where the consecration is to take place two chapels are prepared, a larger one for the consecrating bishop, and a smaller one for the Bishop-elect. And in the larger, upon the altar, prepared in the usual manner, a cross is placed in the middle, and at least four candlesticks. On the ground at the foot of the altar carpets are laid, upon which the Bishop-elect shall prostrate himself, but the Consecrator and the others shall kneel. In an adjacent and suitable place a credence for the Consecrator is also prepared, upon which will be a clean cloth, two candlesticks, basins,

---
* In Liturgy the Feast of an Evangelist is equivalent to that of an Apostle. See note in Appendix, p. I.*

cum suis mantilibus; vas cum aqua benedicta, et aspersorio; thuribulum cum navicella, cochleari, et incenso, si Officium fit in cantu, alias non; ampullæ cum vino, et aqua pro sacrificio; Calix, hostiaria cum hostiis; medulla panis pro abstergendis manibus; sanctum Chrisma.

Item paramenta omnia Pontificalia, coloris tempori et officio Missæ convenientis, videlicet, sandalia, amictus, alba, cingulum, crux pectoralis, stola, tunicella, dalmatica, chirothecæ, planeta, mitra auriphrygiata, annulus Pontificalis, baculus Pastoralis, manipulus et gremiale.

Item paratur faldistorium ornatum pro Consecratore; et tres sedes pro Electo, et duobus Episcopis assistentibus; Missale et Pontificale. Consecrator habeat tres Capellanos ad minus, cum superpelliceis, et duos scutiferos ad credentiam.

In capella vero minore pro Electo, quæ a majore debet esse distincta, paratur altare cum cruce, et duobus candelabris, et super illud Missale, et Pontificale; ac paramenta omnia Pontificalia albi coloris, ut supra pro Consecratore numerata sunt; et ultra illa, pluviale album, et prope altare credentia minor cum mappa munda, et vasis ad abluendum manus, et medulla panis ad extergendum manus, et caput.

Ponuntur etiam octo mappulæ ex duabus cannis panni linei subtilis, per medium scissis in longitudinem, quarum duæ sint longitudinis sex palmorum quælibet, aliæ vero sex æqualis sint quantitatis. Et candelæ saltem octo, unius libræ quælibet, quarum quatuor super altare Consecrantis, duæ super ejus credentiam, et duæ super altare Electi ponuntur.

Annulus cum gemma benedicendus, et Electo tradendus, pecten eburneus. Et pro Offertorio intortitia duo, quatuor librarum quodlibet, duo panes magni, et duo barilia vini; panes et barilia ornentur, duo, videlicet, videantur argentea, et duo aurea,

THE CONSECRATION OF A BISHOP.

and towels for the ablution of the hands, a vessel with holy water, and an aspersorium; and a thurible with boat, spoon and incense, if the office is sung, otherwise this is omitted; cruets with wine and water for the sacrifice; a chalice; the box of hosts; crumbs of bread for the cleansing of the hands; holy chrism. Furthermore, all the pontifical vestments of color suitable to the time and the office of the Mass, namely, sandals and amice, alb. cincture, pectoral cross, stole, tunic, dalmatic, gloves, chasuble, precious mitre, pontifical ring, pastoral staff, maniple and gremial. A faldstool is prepared for the Consecrator and three seats for the Bishop-elect and the two assistant bishops; a Missal and a Pontifical. The Consecrator should have at least three chaplains in surplice, and two acolytes at the credence. In the smaller chapel for the Bishop-Elect, which should be distinct from the larger, an altar is prepared with a cross and two candlesticks, a Missal and a Pontifical, and all the pontifical vestments in white, as enumerated above for the Consecrator, and in addition to these a white cope; near the altar a smaller credence with a clean cloth, vessels for washing the hands, and bread crumbs for cleansing the hands and head. Eight small strips from two rolls of fine linen (cut in lengths through the middle, of which two are each six palms in length, the remaining six being of equal quantity) are prepared, and at least eight candles, each one pound in weight, four of which are placed on the altar of the consecrating bishop, two upon his credence and two upon the altar of the Bishop-elect; a jewelled ring to be blessed and to be given to the Bishop elect; and an ivory comb. For the offertory, two torches four pounds each in weight, two loaves of bread, two small barrels of wine; the bread and the wine are to be ornamented, two to be decorated with silver and two with gold, bearing the

hinc et inde insignia Consecratoris, et Electi habentia, cum capello, vel cruce, vel mitra pro cujusque gradu et dignitate.

Adsint duo ad minus Episcopi assistentes, qui induuntur rochetto, et si sint Regulares, superpelliceo, amictu, stola, pluviali, quæ cum reliquis paramentis sint coloris tempori et officio Missæ congruentis, et mitra simplici alba, et quisque habeat suum Pontificale.

Hora igitur competenti Consecrator, Electus, assistentes Episcopi, et alii, qui consecrationi interesse debent, ad Ecclesiam conveniunt, et Consecrator, facta oratione ante altare, ascendit ad sedem, si sit in Ecclesia sua; vel accedit ad faldistorium in capella sua, juxta cornu Epistolæ præparatum, et ibi de more paratur. Electus vero cum assistentibus Episcopis vadit ad capellam suam, et ibi capit paramenta opportuna, videlicet, si Missa cantatur, amictum, albam, cingulum, stolam in modum Sacerdotis, et pluviale. Si vero Officium legitur, poterit, antequam dicta paramenta accipiat, capere sandalia et legere Psalm. **Quam dilěcta.** etc. Assistentes etiam Episcopi interim sua paramenta prædicta capiunt. Omnibus itaque paratis, Consecrator accedit ante altare, et ibi in medio sedet super falditorium, vertens renes altari. Electus vero cum suo bireto ducitur sic paratus, medius inter assistentes sibi Episcopos paratos, et mitratos, et cum ante Consecratorem pervenerit, nudato capite, illud profunde inclinando, ei reverentiam facit, assistentes vero Episcopi eidem cum mitra caput aliquantulum inclinant.

Tum sedent in sedibus suis, ante Consecratorem, hoc modo: Electus contra faciem Consecratoris, ita ut inter eos sit competens distantia. Antiquior Episcopus assistens ad dexteram Electi, junior ad sinistram; ita tamen, quod ipsi Assistentes ad alterutrum

THE CONSECRATION OF A BISHOP.

escutcheons of the Consecrator and of the Bishop-elect, with hat, or cross, or mitre, according to the grade and dignity of each. At least two assistant bishops shall be present * who are clothed in the rochet, and if they are regulars, in the surplice, the amice, stole, cope and the plain white mitre, and each one has his Pontifical. At a suitable hour the Consecrator, the Bishop-elect, the assistant bishops, and the others who are to be present at the consecration, assemble at the church, and the Consecrator, having prayed before the altar, ascends to his throne if he is in his own diocese, or goes to his chapel, to the faldstool near the Epistle corner, and there is vested as usual. The Bishop-elect, with the assistant bishops goes to his chapel and there puts on the necessary vestments, namely, if the Mass be sung, the amice, alb, cincture and the stole, crossed as it is worn by priests. If, however, the office is read, he can, before he takes the above mentioned vestments, put on the sandals and read the Psalm **Quam Dilecta,** " etc. The assistant bishops, in the meanwhile, put on the vestments as above. All being ready the Consecrator goes to the middle of the altar and there sits on the faldstool with his back to the altar. The Bishop-elect, vested and wearing his biretta, is led between the two assistant bishops vested and mitred, and when he comes before the Consecrator, uncovering his head and profoundly bowing, he makes a reverence to him, the assistant bishops with their mitres on slightly inclining their heads. Then they sit at a little distance from the Consecrator so that the Bishop-elect faces the Consecrator; the senior assistant bishop sits at the right hand of

---

* The presence of three Bishops is required by the ancient Canons, and by the general practice of the Church, but is not essential to the validity of the consecration. By special dispensation priests may assist in lieu of Bishops.

DE CONSECRATIONE ELECTI IN EPISCOPUM.

fácies vertant. Cum sic locuti fuerint, et aliquantulum quieverint, surgunt, Electus sine bireto, et assistentes Episcopi sine mitris, et senior Assistentium versus ad Consecratorem dicit:

R EVERENDISSIME Pater, póstulat sancta mater Ecclésia Cathólica, ut hunc præséntem Presbýterum ad onus Episcopátus sublevétis.

Consecrator dicit:
Habétis mandátum Apostólicum?

Respondet Episcopus senior Assistentium:
Habémus.

Consecrator dicit: **Legátur.**

Tum Notarius Consecratoris accipiens mandatum de manu Episcopi assistentis, legit a principio ad finem. Interim sedent omnes, tectis capitibus. Mandato per Notarium perlecto, Consecrator dicit: **Deo grátias.**

Vel, si consecratio fit vigore litterarum Apostolicarum, per quas etiam juramenti per Electum præstandi receptio Consecratori committitur, litteris ipsis lectis, antequam Consecrator aliud dicat, Electus de sede sua veniens coram Consecratore genuflectit; et legit juramentum de verbo ad verbum, juxta tenorem commissionis prædictæ præstandum, in hunc modum, videlicet:

the Bishop-elect, the junior at his left, facing one another. When they shall have thus been seated, after a short pause they rise, the Bishop-elect without his biretta and the assistant bishops without their mitres, and the senior assistant, turned to the Consecrator, says:

MOST Reverend Father, our holy Mother the Catholic Church, asks that you promote this priest here present to the burden of the episcopate.

The Consecrator says:

Have you the Apostolic Mandate?

The senior assistant bishop answers:

We have.

The Consecrator says: **Let it be read.**

Then the notary of the Consecrator, taking the mandate from the assistant bishop, reads it from the beginning to the end; in the meanwhile all sit with heads covered. The mandate having been read, the Consecrator says: **Thanks be to God.**

Or, if the consecration is made by virtue of Apostolic letters, by which even the reception of the oath to be made by the Bishop-elect is committed to the Consecrator, these letters being read, before the Consecrator says anything else, the Bishop-elect coming from his seat, kneels before the Consecrator and reads, word for word, the oath to be taken according to the tenor of the aforesaid commission, in this manner, viz:

FORMA JURAMENTI.

E GO N. Eléctus Ecclésiæ N. ab hac hora in ántea obédiens ero beáto Petro Apóstolo, sanctǽque Románæ Ecclésiæ, et Beatíssimo Patri N. Papæ N. suísque successóribus canónice intrántibus. Papátum Románum, adjútor eis ero ad retinéndum, et defendéndum, salvo meo órdine. Jura, honóres, privilégia, et auctoritátem sanctæ Románæ Ecclésiæ, Dómini nostri Papæ et successórum prædictórum, conserváre, deféndere, augére, et promovére curábo. Régulas sanctórum Patrum, decréta, ordinatiónes, seu dispositiónes, reservatiónes, provisiónes, et mandáta Apostólica, totis víribus observábo, et fáciam ab áliis observári. Vocátus ad sýnodum, véniam, nisi præpedítus fúero canónica præpeditióne. Apostolórum límina síngulis decénniis personáliter per me ipsum visitábo ; et Beatíssimo Patri nostro, N. ac successóribus præfátis, ratiónem reddam de toto meo pastoráli offício, ac de rebus ómnibus ad meæ Ecclésiæ statum, ad cleri et

FORM OF OATH.

I N., elected to the Church of N., from this hour henceforward will be obedient to Blessed Peter the Apostle, and to the holy Roman Church, and to our Holy Father, Pope N. and to his successors canonically elected. I will assist them to retain and to defend the Roman Papacy without detriment to my order. I shall take care to preserve, to defend, increase and promote the rights, honors, privileges and authority of the holy Roman Church, of our lord, the Pope, and of his aforesaid successors. I shall observe with all my strength, and shall cause to be observed by others, the rules of the holy Fathers, the Apostolic decrees, ordinances or dispositions, reservations, provisions and mandates. I shall come when called to a Synod, unless prevented by a canonical impediment. I shall make personally the visit *ad limina apostolorum* every ten years, and I shall render to our Holy Father, Pope N.,and to his aforesaid successors an account of my whole pastoral office, and of all things pertaining in any manner whatsoever to the state of my Church, to the discipline of the clergy and the people, and finally to the salvation

FORMA JURAMENTI.

pópuli disciplínam, animárum dénique, quæ meæ fídei tráditæ sunt, salútem quovis modo pertinéntibus: et vicíssim mandáta Apostólica humíliter recípiam, et quam diligentíssime éxsequar. Quod si legítimo impediménto deténtus fúero, præfáta ómnia adimplébo per certum Núntium ad hoc speciále mandátum habéntem, diœcesánum sacerdótem, vel per áliquem álium presbýterum sæculárem, vel regulárem, spectátæ probitátis, et religiónis, de supradíctis ómnibus plene instrúctum. Possessiónes vero ad mensam meam pertinéntes non vendam, nec donábo, neque impignorábo, nec de novo infeudábo, vel áliquo modo alienábo, etiam cum consénsu Capítuli Ecclésiæ meæ, inconsúlto Románo Pontífice. Et si ad áliquam alienatiónem devénero, pœnas in quadam super hoc édita constitutióne conténtas, eo ipso incúrrere volo.

Consecrator in gremio suo librum Evangeliorum ambabus manibus apertum tenens, inferiore parte libri Electo versa, ab eo præstationem hujusmodi juramenti recipit, Electo adhuc coram eo genuflexo dicente:

Sic me Deus ádjuvet, et hæc sancta Dei Evangélia.

of the souls which are entrusted to me: and in turn I shall receive humbly the apostolic mandates and execute them as diligently as possible. But if I shall be detained by legitimate impediment, I shall fulfil all the aforesaid things through a designated delegate having a special mandate for this purpose, a priest of my diocese, or through some other secular or regular priest of known probity and religion, fully informed concerning the above-named things. I shall not sell, nor give, nor mortgage the possessions belonging to my *mensa*,* nor shall I enfeoff them anew or alienate them in any manner, even with the consent of the chapter of my Church, without consulting the Roman Pontiff. And if through me any such alienation shall occur, I wish, by the very fact, to incur the punishments contained in the constitution published concerning this matter.

The Consecrator, holding in his lap with both hands the books of the Gospels, opened towards the Bishop-elect, receives from him this oath, the Bishop-elect still kneeling before him, saying:

So help me God and these Holy Gospels of God.

---

* By the *mensa* is understood the real estate or investments set aside for the proper support of the Bishop.

Et ipsum textum Evangeliorum ambabus manibus tangente, tum, non prius, dicit Consecrator :

Deo grátias.

Deinde Electo, et Assistentibus in locis suis (ut dictum est) sedentibus. Consecrator intelligibili voce legit sequentem examinationem, quæ legi debet semper, sicut jacet, in singulari, etiam si plures simul examinentur. Assistentes vero Episcopi submissa voce dicunt quæcumque dixerit Consecrator, et omnes debent tunc mitras tenere, et sedere.

EXAMEN.

ANTIQUA sanctórum Patrum institútio docet, et præcipit, ut is qui ad Episcopátus órdinem elígitur, ántea diligentíssime examinétur cum omni caritáte, de fide sanctæ Trinitátis: et interrogétur de divérsis causis, et móribus, quæ huic regímini cóngruunt, ac necessária sunt retinéri secúndum Apóstoli dictum: Manus némini cito imposúeris. Et ut étiam is, qui ordinándus est, erudiátur, quáliter sub hoc regímine constitútum opórteat conversári in Ecclésia Dei ; et ut irreprehensíbiles sint, qui ei manus ordinatiónis impónunt. Eádem ítaque auctoritáte et præcépto, interrogámus te,

He touches with both hands the text of the Gospels and then, and not before, the Consecrator says:

Thanks be to God.

Then the Bishop-elect and the assistants being seated, the Consecrator reads in an audible voice the following examination, which should always be read as it is written, in the singular, even if many are examined together. The assistant bishops say in a lower voice whatsoever the Consecrator says, and all should retain their mitres and be seated..

EXAMINATION.

THE ancient rule of the holy Fathers teaches and ordains that he who is chosen to the order of bishop, shall be with all charity examined diligently beforehand concerning his faith in the Holy Trinity, and shall be questioned concerning the different objects and rules which pertain to this government and are to be observed, according to the word of the apostle: "impose hands hastily on no man." This is done in order that he who is to be ordained may be instructed how it behooveth one placed under this rule to conduct himself in the Church of God, and also that they may be blameless who impose on him the hands of ordination. Therefore by the same authority and commandment, with

dilectíssime frater, caritáte sincéra, si omnem prudéntiam tuam, quantum tua capax est natúra, divínæ Scriptúræ sénsibus accommodáre volúeris.

Tum Electus aliquantulum assurgens, detecto capite, respondet:

Ita ex toto corde volo in ómnibus consentíre, et obedíre.

Et hoc servabit ad omnes alias responsiones sequentes. Et si plures Electi fuerint, successive quisque sic respondet.

Interrogat Consecrator.

VIS ea, quæ ex divínis Scriptúris intélligis, plebem, cui ordinándus es, et verbis docére, et exémplis? R. Volo.

Interrogatio.

Vis traditiónes orthodoxórum Patrum, ac Decretáles sanctæ et Apóstolicæ Sedis Constitutiónes veneránter suscípere, docére, ac serváre? R. Volo.

Interrogatio.

Vis beáto Petro Apóstolo, cui a Deo data est potéstas ligándi, ac solvéndi; ejúsque Vicário Dómino nostro, Dómino N. Papæ N. suísque successóribus, Románis Pontifícibus, fidem, subjectiónem,

sincere charity, we ask you, dearest brother, if you desire to make your conduct harmonize, as far as your nature allows, with the meaning of the divine Scripture.

Then the Bishop-elect, rising slightly, with uncovered head, answers:

With my whole heart I wish in all things to consent and obey.

And he will act in like manner when making all the other responses that follow, and if there are many Bishops-elect, each one will answer thus in turn.

The Consecrator interrogates.

Q. Will you teach the people for whom you are ordained, both by words and by example, the things you understand from the divine Scriptures?

R. I will.

Q. Will you receive, keep and teach with reverence the traditions of the orthodox fathers and the decretal constitutions of the Holy and Apostolic See?

R. I will.

Q. Will you exhibit in all things fidelity, submission, obedience, according to canonical authority, to Blessed Peter the Apostle, to whom was given by God the power of binding and of loosing, and

et obediéntiam, secúndum canónicam auctoritátem, per ómnia exhibére? R. Volo.

Interrogatio.

Vis mores tuos ab omni malo temperáre, et quantum póteris, Dómino adjuvánte, ad omne bonum commutáre? R. Vo o.

Interrogatio.

Vis castitátem, et sobrietátem cum Dei auxílio custodíre, et docére? R. Volo.

Interrogatio.

Vis semper in divínis esse negótiis mancipátus, et a terrénis negótiis, vel lucris túrpibus aliénus, quantum te humána fragílitas consénserit posse? R. Volo.

Interrogatio.

Vis humilitátem, et patiéntiam in teípso custodíre et álios simíliter docére? R. Volo.

Interrogatio.

Vis paupéribus, et peregrínis, omnibúsque indigéntibus esse propter nomen Dómini affábilis, et miséricors? R. Volo.

Tunc dicit ei Consecrator:

HÆC ómnia, et cétera bona tríbuat tibi Dóminus, et custódiat te, atque corróboret in omni bonitáte.

Et respondent omnes: Amen.

EXAMINATION.

to his Vicar our Holy Father, Pope **N.** and to his successors the Roman Pontiffs?

R. I will.

Q. Will you refrain in all your ways from evil and, as far as you are able, with the help of the Lord, direct them to every good?

R. I will.

Q. Will you observe and teach, with the help of God, chastity and sobriety?

R. I will.

Q. Will you, as far as your human frailty shall allow, always be given up to divine affairs and abstain from worldly matters or sordid gains?

R. I will.

Q. Will you yourself observe, and likewise teach others to observe humility and patience?

R. I will.

Q. Will you, for the Lord's sake, be affable and merciful to the poor and to pilgrims and all those in need?

R. I will.

Then the Consecrator says to him:

MAY the Lord bestow upon thee all these things and every other good thing, and preserve thee and strengthen thee in all goodness.

And all answer: Amen.

Interrogatio.

CREDIS, secúndum intelligéntiam, et capacitátem sensus tui, sanctam Trinitátem, Patrem, et Fílium, et Spíritum sanctum, unum Deum omnipoténtem, totámque in sancta Trinitáte Deitátem, coëssentiálem, consubstantiálem, coætérnam, et coomnipoténtem, uníus voluntátis, potestátis, et majestátis, creatórem ómnium creaturárum, a quo ómnia, per quem ómnia, et in quo ómnia, quæ sunt in cœlo, et in terra, visibília, et invisibília, corporália, et spirituália? R. Asséntio, et ita credo.

Interrogatio

Credis síngulam quamque in sancta Trinitáte persónam unum Deum, verum, plenum, et perféctum? R. Credo.

Interrogatio.

Credis ipsum Fílium Dei, Verbum Dei æternáliter natum de Patre, consubstantiálem, coomnipoténtem, et coæquálem per ómnia Patri in divinitáte, temporáliter natum de Spíritu sancto ex María semper Vírgine, cum ánima rationáli, duas habéntem nativitátes, unam ex Patre ætérnam, álteram ex matre temporálem, Deum verum, et hóminem verum, próprium in utráque natúra, atque perféctum, non adoptívum, nec phantasmáticum, sed únicum, et unum Fílium Dei in duábus, et

EXAMINATION.

Q. Do you believe, according to your understanding and the capacity of your mind, in the Holy Trinity, the Father and the Son and the Holy Ghost, one God almighty and the whole Godhead, in the Holy Trinity coessential, consubstantial, coeternal, and coömnipotent, of one will, power and majesty, the Creator of all creatures, by whom are all things, through whom are all things, and in whom are all things in heaven and on earth, visible and invisible, corporeal and spiritual?

R. I assent and do so believe.

Q. Do you believe each single person of the Holy Trinity is one God, true, full and perfect?

R. I do believe.

Q. Do you believe in the Son of God, the Word of God eternally begotten of the Father, consubstantial, coömnipotent and coequal in all things to the Father in divinity, born in time of the Holy Ghost from Mary ever Virgin, with a rational soul, having two nativities, one eternal from the Father, the other temporal from the Mother, true God and true Man, proper and perfect in both natures, not the adopted nor the fantastic, but the sole and only Son of God in two natures and of two natures, but in the singleness of one person, incapable of

ex duábus natúris, sed in uníus persónæ
singularitáte, impassíbilem, et immortálem
divinitáte, sed in humanitáte pro nobis, et
pro salúte nostra passum vera carnis pas-
sióne, et sepúltum, ac tértia die resurgén-
tem a mórtuis vera carnis resurrectióne;
die quadragésimo post resurrectiónem
cum carne, qua resurréxit, et ánima as-
cendísse ad cœlum, et sedére ad déxteram
Patris; inde ventúrum judicáre vivos, et
mórtuos; et redditúrum unicuíque secúndum ópera sua, sive bona fúerint, sive
mala? R. Asséntio, et ita per ómnia
credo.

Interrogatio.

Credis étiam Spíritum sanctum, plenum,
et perféctum, verúmque Deum, a Patre et
Fílio procedéntem, coæquálem, et coëssentiálem, coomnipoténtem, et coætérnum
per ómnia Patri, et Fílio? R. Credo.

Interrogatio.

Credis hanc sanctam Trinitátem, non
tres Deos, sed unum Deum omnipoténtem,
ætérnum, invisibílem, et inconimutábilem?
R. Credo.

Interrogatio.

Credis sanctam, cathólicam, et apostóli-
cam, unam esse veram Ecclésiam, in qua
unum datur verum baptísma, et vera óm-

suffering, and immortal in his divinity, but Who suffered in his humanity for us and for our salvation, with real suffering of the flesh, and was buried, and, rising on the third day from the dead with a true resurrection of the flesh, on the fortieth day after resurrection, with the flesh wherein he rose and with his soul, ascended into Heaven and sitteth at the right hand of the Father, thence to come to judge the living and the dead, and to render to everyone according to his works as they shall have been good or bad?

R. I assent and so in all things do I believe.

Q. Do you believe also in the Holy Ghost full and perfect and true God, proceeding from the Father and the Son, coequal and coessential, coömnipotent and coeternal in all things with the Father and the Son?

R. I believe.

Q. Do you believe that this Holy Trinity is not three Gods, but one God, almighty, eternal, invisible and unchangeable?

R. I believe.

Q. Do you believe that the holy Catholic and Apostolic Church is the one true

nium remíssio peccatórum ? ℟. Credo.

Interrogatio.

Anathematízas étiam omnem hǽresim, extolléntem se advérsus hanc sanctam Ecclésiam cathólicam ? ℟. Anathematízo.

Interrogatio.

Credis étiam veram resurrectiónem ejúsdem carnis, quam nunc gestas, et vitam ætérnam ? ℟. Credo.

Interrogatió.

Credis étiam novi, et véteris Testaménti, legis, et Prophetárum, et Apostolórum, unum esse auctórem Deum, ac Dóminum omnipoténtem ? ℟. Credo.

Postea Consecrator dicit:

HÆC tibi fides augeátur a Dómino, ad veram, et ætérnam beatúdinem, dilectíssime frater in Christo.

Et respondent omnes: Amen.

Expleto itaque examine, præfati assistentes Episcopi ducunt Electum ad Consecratorem, coram quo genuflexus, ejus manum reverenter osculatur. Tunc Consecrator, deposita mitra, cum ministris ad altare conversus, facit, solito more Confes-

EXAMINATION.

Church in which there is but one true baptism and the true remission of all sins?

℟ I believe.

℣ Do you also anathematize every heresy that shall arise against this holy Catholic Church?

℟ I do anathematize it.

℣ Do you believe also in the true resurrection of this same flesh of yours, and in life everlasting?

℟ I do believe.

℣ Do you believe also that God and the Lord Almighty is the sole author of the New and Old Testaments, of the Law, and of the Prophets, and of the Apostles?

℟ I do believe.

Afterwards the Consecrator says:

MAY this faith be increased in thee, by the Lord, unto true and eternal happiness, dearest brother in Christ.

All answer: Amen.

The examination being finished, the aforesaid assistant bishops lead the Bishop-elect to the Consecrator, whose hand is reverently kissed by the Bishop-elect kneeling. Then the Consecrator, laying aside his mitre, and turning towards the altar with the ministers, says in the usual manner the Confession, the Bishop-elect remaining at his left hand, and

16 DE CONSECRATIONE ELECTI IN EPISCOPUM.

sionem, Electo a sinistris ejus manente; et omnes Episcopi ante sedes suas stantes faciunt similiter Confessionem cum Capellanis suis. Facta itaque Confessione, Consecrator ascendit ad altare, et osculatur illud, et Evangelium in Missa dicendum; et incensat altare, more solito. Deinde vadit ad sedem suam, vel faldistorium, et procedit in Missa usque ad **Allelúia,** sive ultimum Versum Tractus, vel Sequentiæ exclusive.

Si vero Missa legitur, osculato altari, et Evangelio, omissa incensatione, omnia prædicta legit in altari, et illis dictis, sive Missa legatur, sive cantetur, redit cum mitra ad sedendum in faldistorio, quod ante medium altaris sibi reponitur.

Episcopi vero assistentes ducunt Electum ad capellam suam, et ibi deposito pluviali, Acolythi induunt illum sandalia, ipso Psalmos, et Orationes consuetas legente, si prius illa non acceperit. Tum accipit crucem pectoralem, et stola ei aptatur, ut ab humeris dependeat. Deinde tunicella, dalmatica, casula, et manipulo induitur; quibus indutus accedit ad suum altari, ubi stans in medio medius inter Episcopos assistentes, detecto capite legit totum Officium Missæ, usque ad **Allelúia,** sive ultimum Versum Tractus, vel Sequentiæ exclusive; nec vertit se ad populum cum dicit, **Dóminus vobiscum,** ut in aliis Missis fieri solet.

Propter ordinationes Episcoporum numquam mutatur Officium diei; dicitur tamen post Collectam diei pro Officio Consecrationis, Collecta pro Electo, sub uno **Per Dóminum nostrum,** etc.

THE CONSECRATION OF A BISHOP. 16

the bishops standing before their seats say in like manner the Confession, with their chaplains. Having finished the Confession the Consecrator ascends to the altar, kisses it and the Gospel to be said in the Mass, and incenses the altar in the usual manner. Then he goes to his throne or faldstool and proceeds with the Mass up to the Alleluia, or the last verse of the tract or sequence exclusive.

If Mass is read, however, having kissed the altar and the Gospel, the incensation being omitted, he reads as above from the Missal at the altar, after which, whether the Mass is read or sung, he returns with his mitre on to the faldstool, placed for him before the middle of the altar.

The assistant bishops lead the Bishop-elect to his chapel, and there having laid aside the cope, acolytes put on his sandals, if he has not already done so, he reading the usual psalms and prayers. Then he receives the pectoral cross and adjusts the stole in such a manner that it may hang from his shoulders. After that, he is vested with the tunic, dalmatic, chasuble and maniple, and then advances to his altar, where, standing between the assistant bishops, with uncovered head, he reads the whole office of the Mass up to the Alleluia, or the last verse of the tract or sequence exclusive. He does not turn around to the people when he says The Lord be with you, as is wont to be done in other Masses.

The office of the day is never changed on account of the ordination of bishops. But after the collect of the day, a collect for the Bishop-elect is said under one Through Christ Our Lord, etc.

DE CONSECRATIONE ELECTI IN EPISCOPUM.

ORATIO.

ADESTO supplicatiónibus nostris, omnípotens Deus, ut quod humilitátis nostræ geréndum est ministério, tuæ virtútis impleátur efféctu. Per Dóminum nostrum Jesum Christum Fílium tuum: Qui tecum vivit, et regnat in unitáte Spíritus sancti Deus, per ómnia sǽcula sæculórum. ℟. Amen.

Finito Graduali, si Allelúia dicitur, alioquin dicto Tractu vel Sequentia, usque ad ultimum Versum exclusive, Consecrator accedit ad faldistorium ante medium altaris, et ibi sedet cum mitra; assistentes vero Episcopi iterum ducunt Electum ad Consecratorem, cui Electus, deposito bireto, caput profunde inclinans humilem reverentiam facit: Assistentes vero cum mitris se aliquantulum inclinantes, etiam Consecratorem venerantur. Tum sedent omnes, ut prius; et Consecrator sedens cum mitra, versus ad illum, dicit:

EPISCOPUM opórtet judicáre, interpretári, consecráre, ordináre, offérre, baptizáre, et confirmáre.

THE CONSECRATION OF A BISHOP. 17

PRAYER.

ATTEND to our supplications, Almighty God, so that what is to be performed by our humble ministry may be fulfilled by the effect of Thy power. Through Our Lord Jesus Christ Thy Son, who liveth and reigneth with Thee in the unity of the Holy Ghost, world without end. ℟ Amen.

The Gradual being finished, if the Alleluia *is said, otherwise the tract or sequence up to the last verse exclusively being read, the Consecrator goes to the faldstool before the middle of the altar and there sits with his mitre on;* * *the assistant bishops again lead the Bishop-elect to the Consecrator, to whom the Bishop-elect, having laid aside his biretta,* † *profoundly bending his head, makes an humble reverence; the assistants with their mitres on, and bowing slightly, also make a reverence to the Consecrator, then all sit as before, and the Consecrator, sitting with his mitre on, turned towards the Bishop-elect, says:*

A bishop judges, interprets, consecrates, ordains, offers, baptizes and confirms.

---

* The wearing of the mitre indicates the exercise of episcopal authority. By bearing this in mind the importance of these Rubrics, concerning the putting on and removal of the mitre, will be better appreciated.

† It will be observed that the Elect removes his biretta as a sign of respect for the superior authority of the Bishop.

18 DE CONSECRATIONE ELECTI IN EPISCOPUM.

Deinde omnibus surgentibus, Consecrator stans cum mitra, dicit ad circumstantes:

OREMUS, fratres caríssimi, ut huic Elécto utilitáti Ecclésiæ próvidens benígnitas omnipoténtis Dei grátiæ suæ tríbuat largitátem. Per Christum Dóminum nostrum. R. Amen.

Et mox Consecrator ante faldistorium suum, et assistentes Episcopi ante sedes suas cum mitris procumbunt; Electus vero prosternit se a sinistris Consecratoris; ministri etiam, atque alii omnes genuflectunt.

Tum cantor, vel, si officium fit legendo, Consecrator incipit Litanias, dicens, **Kýrie eléison,** etc., prosequendo totas prout infra in Appendice p. 1.*

Postquam autem dictum fuerit:

Ut ómnibus fidélibus defúnctis, etc.
R. Te rogámus, audi nos.

Consecrator ab accubitu surgens, ad Electum conversus, baculum Pastoralem cum sinistra tenens, dicit sub voce Litaniarum, primo:

Ut hunc præséntem Eléctum bene ✠ dícere dignéris.
R. Te rogámus, audi nos.

Secundo dicit:

Ut hunc præséntem Eléctum bene ✠ dícere, et sancti ✠ ficáre dignéris.
R. Te rogámus, audi nos.

Then all rising, the Consecrator, standing with his mitre on, says to those surrounding him:

LET us pray, dearest brethren, that the kindness of the Almighty God consulting the utility of His Church, may bestow the abundance of His grace upon this Elect. Through Christ Our Lord. ℟. Amen.

And then the Consecrator before his faldstool, and the assistant bishops before theirs, all with their mitres on, prostrate themselves. The Bishop-elect, however, prostrates himself at the left of the Consecrator; the ministers and all others kneel. Then the chanter, or if the office is read, the Consecrator, beginning the litanies, says:

Lord have mercy on us, going through the entire litanies. After the petition. **That Thou wouldst vouchsafe to all the faithful departed,** etc. ℟. **We beseech Thee, hear us,** has been said.

The Consecrator, rising and turning towards the Bishop-elect, holding in his left hand the pastoral staff, says in the tone of the litanies, first:

That Thou wouldst vouchsafe to ✠ bless this Elect here present.
℟. **We beseech Thee, hear us.**

He says a second time:

That Thou wouldst vouchsafe to ✠bless and ✠sanctify this Elect here present.
℟. **We beseech Thee, hear us.**

* See Appendix. p. I. *

Tertio dicit:

Ut hunc præséntem Eléctum bene dícere, et sancti ✠ ficáre, et conse ✠ cráre dignéris.

℟. **Te rogámus, audi nos.**

Producendo semper signum crucis super illum; idemque faciunt, et dicunt assistentes Episcopi, genuflexi tamen permanentes.

Deinde iterum procumbit Consecrator: et cantor, seu ipse, qui prius dixit, eas prosequitur usque ad finem.

Ut nos exaudíre dígneris, etc.

Quibus finitis, surgunt omnes; et Consecratore ante faldistorium suum cum mitra stante, Electus coram eo genuflectit.

Tum Consecrator, accepto libro Evangeliorum, illum apertum, adjuvantibus Episcopis assistentibus, nihil dicens, imponit super cervicem, et scapulas Electi, ita quod inferior pars libri cervicem capitis Electi tangat, littera ex parte inferiori manente, quem unus ex Capellanis Electi, post ipsum genuflexus, quousque liber ipse eidem Electo in manus tradendus sit, continue sustinet.

Deinde Consecrator et assistentes Episcopi ambabus manibus caput Consecrandi tangunt dicentes:

Accipe Spíritum sanctum.

Quo facto, Consecrator stans, deposita mitra dicit:

THE CONSECRATION OF A BISHOP.

He says a third time

That Thou wouldst vouchsafe ✠ bless ✠ and sanctify and ✠ consecrate this Elect here present.
R. **We beseech Thee, hear us.**

Meanwhile always making the sign of the cross over him, and the assistant bishops do and say the same thing, remaining kneeling, however.

Then the Consecrator again prostrates himself, and the chanter, or he who began the litanies, continues them to the end.

That Thou wouldst vouchsafe, etc.
R. **We beseech Thee, hear us.**

The litany finished, all rise; and the Consecrator stands with his mitre on before his faldstool, the Bishop-elect kneeling before him.

Then the Consecrator, with the aid of the assistant bishops, taking the open book of the Gospels, saying nothing, lays it upon the neck and shoulders of the Bishop-elect, so that the printed page touches the neck. One of the chaplains kneels behind, supporting the book until it must be given into the hands of the Bishop-elect.

Then the Consecrator and the assistant bishops touch with both hands the head of the one to be consecrated saying: *

Receive the Holy Ghost.

This being done, the Consecrator, standing and laying aside his mitre, says:

---

* The imposition of hands with prayer is the essential rite by which Episcopal power is conferred.

PROPITIARE, Dómine, supplicatiónibus nostris, et inclináto super hunc fámulum tuum cornu grátiæ sacerdotális, bene ✠ dictiónis tuæ in eum effúnde virtútem. Per Dóminum nostrum Jesum Christum Fílium tuum : Qui tecum vivit, et regnat in unitáte Spíritus sancti Deus.

Deinde, extensis manibus ante pectus, dicit:

PER ómnia sǽcula sæculórum.
R. Amen.
V. Dóminus vobíscum.
R. Et cum spíritu tuo.
V. Sursum corda.
R. Habémus ad Dóminum.
V. Grátias agámus Dómino Deo nostro.
R. Dignum et justum est.

Vere dignum et justum est, æquum et salutáre, nos tibi semper, et ubíque grátias ágere, Dómine sancte, Pater omnípotens, ætérne Deus, honor ómnium dignitátum, quæ glóriæ tuæ sacris famulántur ordínibus. Deus, qui Móysen fámulum tuum secréti familiáris affátu, inter cétera coeléstis documénta cultúræ, de habitu quoque induménti sacerdotális instítuens, eléctum

BE propitious, O Lord, to our supplications, and inclining the horn of sacerdotal grace above this Thy servant, pour out upon him the power of Thy ✠ blessing. Through Our Lord Jesus Christ, who liveth and reigneth with Thee in the unity of the Holy Ghost, God.

Then extending his hands before his breast, he says:

WORLD without end.
R. Amen.
V. The Lord be with you.
R. And with thy spirit.
V. Lift up your hearts.
R. We have them lifted up to the Lord.
V. Let us give thanks to the Lord our God.
R. It is worthy and just.

It is truly worthy and just, right and profitable unto salvation that we should at all times and in all places give thanks unto Thee, O holy Lord, Father Almighty, Eternal God, honor of all dignities which serve unto Thy glory in sacred orders. To Thee O God, who, in the secret communings of familiar intercourse, giving instruction unto Moses Thy servant, concerning, among other branches of divine worship, the nature of sacerdotal vesture, didst order that Aaron, Thy chosen one,

Aaron mýstico amíctu vestíri inter sacra jussísti, ut intelligéntiæ sensum de exémplis priórum cáperet secutúra postéritas, ne erudítio doctrínæ tuæ ulli deésset ætáti. Cum et apud véteres reveréntiam ipsa significatiónum spécies obtinéret, et apud nos certióra essent experiménta rerum, quam ænígmata figurárum. Illíus namque Sacerdótii anterióris hábitus, nostræ mentis ornátus est, et Pontificálem glóriam non jam nobis honor comméndat véstium, sed splendor animárum. Quia et illa, quæ tunc carnálibus blandiebántur obtútibus, ea pótius, quæ in ipsis erant, intelligénda poscébant. Et idcírco huic fámulo tuo, quem ad summi Sacerdótii ministérium elegísti, hanc, quǽsumus Dómine, grátiam largiáris, ut quidquid illa velámina in fulgóre auri, in nitóre gemmárum, et in multímodi óperis varietáte signábant, hoc in ejus móribus actibúsque claréscat. Comple in Sacerdóte tuo ministérii tui summam, et ornaméntis totíus

should be clad in mystic robes during the sacred functions, so that succeeding generations might be enlightened by the examples of their predecessors, lest the knowledge derived from Thy instruction should be wanting in any age. Since, indeed, with the ancients, the very appearance of symbols would obtain reverence, and with us there would be the experience of the things themselves more certain than the mysteries of figures. For the adornment of our minds fulfils what was expressed by the outward vesture of that ancient priesthood, and now brightness of souls rather than splendor of raiment commends the pontifical glory unto us. Because even those things which then were sightly unto the eyes of the flesh, demanded rather that the eyes of the spirit should understand the things they signified. And therefore we beseech Thee, O Lord, give bountifully this grace to this Thy servant, whom Thou hast chosen to the ministry of the supreme priesthood, so that what things soever those vestments signify by the refulgence of gold, the splendor of jewels, and the variety of diversified works, these may shine forth in his character and his actions. Fill up in Thy priest the perfection of Thy ministry and sanctify

DE CONSECRATIONE ELECTI IN EPISCOPUM.

glorificatiónis instrúctum, cœléstis unguénti rore sanctífica.

Si in Romana curia fit Consecratio, Subdiaconus Apostolicus, vel unus ex Capellanis Pontificis ligat caput Electi cum una ex longioribus mappulis, de octo superius dictis, et Consecrator, flexis genibus, versus ad altare incipit, ceteris prosequentibus, Hymnum:

Veni Creátor Spíritus.

Et dicitur usque ad finem prouti habetur in Appendice. p. 7*.

Finito primo Versu, surgit Pontifex; et sedet in faldistorio ante medium altaris; capit mitram; deponit annulum et chirothecas; resumit annulum, et imponitur ei gremiale a ministris. Tum pollicem suum dexterum intingit in sanctum Chrisma, et caput Electi coram se genuflexi inungit, formans primo signum crucis per totam coronam, deinde reliquum coronæ liniendo, interim dicens:

UNGATUR, et consecrétur caput tuum, cœlésti benedictióne, in órdine Pontificáli.

Et producens manu dextera tertio signum crucis super caput Electi, dicit:

In nómine Pa ✠ tris, et Fí ✠ lii, et Spíritus ✠ sancti.
R. Amen.

with the dew of Thy heavenly ointment this Thy servant decked out with the ornaments of all beauty.

If the consecration is performed in the Roman *curia*, the Apostolic Subdeacon or one of the pontifical chaplains binds the head of the Bishop-elect with one of the longer cloths from the eight mentioned above, and the Consecrator, prostrate on both knees, turned towards the altar, begins the Hymn, **Come Holy Ghost, Creator, come,** * the others continuing it unto the end.

At the conclusion of the first verse, the bishop rises and sits on the faldstool before the middle of the altar, takes his mitre, lays aside his ring and gloves, puts on the ring again and receives the gremial from the ministers. Then he dips the thumb of his right hand in the holy chrism and anoints the head of the Bishop-elect kneeling before him, making first the sign of the cross on the crown, then anointing the rest of the crown, saying in the meanwhile:

MAY thy head be anointed and consecrated by heavenly benediction in the pontifical order.

And making with his right hand, the sign of the cross three times over the head of the Elect, he says:

✠ In the name of the ✠ Father, and of the Son, and of the Holy ✠ Ghost.
R. Amen.

---

* See Appendix, p. 7*.

℣. Pax tibi.
℟. Et cum spíritu tuo.

Et si plures sint consecrandi, hoc in persona cujuslibet singulariter repetit.

Expleta unctione, Pontifex pollicem cum medulla panis paululum abstergit; et finito Hymno prædicto, deposita mitra, surgit, et in pristina voce prosequitur, dicens:

HOC, Dómine, copióse in caput ejus ínfluat, hoc in oris subjécta decúrrat; hoc in totíus córporis extréma descéndat, ut tui Spíritus virtus et interióra ejus répleat, et exterióra circúmtegat. Abúndet in eo constántia fídei, púritas dilectiónis, sincéritas pacis. Sint speciósi múnere tuo pedes ejus ad evangelizándum pacem, ad evangelizándum bona tua. Da ei, Dómine, ministérium reconciliatiónis in verbo, et in factis, in virtúte signórum et prodigiórum. Sit sermo ejus, et prædicátio, non in persuasibílibus humánæ sapiéntiæ verbis, sed in ostensióne spíritus et virtútis. Da ei, Dómine, claves regni cœlórum ut utátur, non gloriétur potestáte, quam tríbuis in ædificatiónem, non in

℣. Peace be with thee.
℟. And with thy spirit.

And if several are to be consecrated, he repeats this to each separately.

Having completed the anointing, the bishop cleanses his thumb somewhat with bread crumbs, and the above-mentioned hymn having been finished, he lays aside his mitre, rises and continues in the same tone as before, saying:

MAY this, O Lord, flow abundantly upon his head, may this run down upon his cheeks, may this extend unto the extemities of his whole body, so that inwardly he may be filled with the power of Thy spirit, and outwardly may be clothed with that same spirit. May constant faith, pure love, sincere piety abound in him. May his feet by Thy gift be beautiful for announcing the glad tidings of peace, for announcing the glad tidings of Thy good things. Grant to him, O Lord, the ministry of reconciliation in word and in deed, in the power of signs and of wonders. Let his speech and his preaching be not in the persuasive words of human wisdom, but in the showing of the spirit and of power. Give to him, O Lord, the keys of the kingdom of Heaven, so that he may make use of, not boast of the power

destructiónem. Quodcúmque ligáverit super terram, sit ligátum et in cœlis, et quodcúmque sólverit super terram, sit solútum et in cœlis. Quorum retinúerit peccáta, reténta sint, et quorum remíserit, tu remíttas. Qui maledíxerit ei, sit ille maledíctus, et qui benedíxerit ei, benedictiónibus repleátur. Sit fidélis servus, et prudens, quem constítuas tu, Dómine, super famíliam tuam, ut det illis cibum in témpore opportúno, et exhíbeat omnem hóminem perféctum. Sit sollicitúdine ímpiger, sit spíritu fervens, óderit supérbiam, humilitátem ac veritátem díligat, neque eam umquam déserat, aut láudibus aut timóre superátus. Non ponat lucem ténebras, nec ténebras lucem: non dicat malum bonum, nec bonum malum. Sit sapiéntibus et insipiéntibus débitor; ut fructum de proféctu ómnium consequátur. Tríbuas ei, Dómine, cáthedram Episcopálem, ad regéndum Ecclésiam tuam, et plebem sibi commíssam. Sis ei auctóritas, sis ei potéstas, sis ei firmitas. Multíplica super eum bene ✠ dictiónem et grátiam tuam: ut ad exorándam semper misericór-

THE CONSECRATION OF A BISHOP.

which Thou bestowest unto edification, not unto destruction. Whatsoever he shall bind upon earth, let it be bound likewise in heaven, and whatsoever he shall loose upon earth, let it likewise be loosed in heaven. Whose sins he shall retain, let them be retained, and do Thou remit the sins of whomsoever he shall remit. Let him who shall curse him, himself be accursed, and let him who shall bless him be filled with blessings. Let him be the faithful and prudent servant whom Thou dost set, O Lord, over Thy household, so that he may give them food in due season, and prove himself a perfect man. May he be untiring in his solicitude, fervent in spirit. May he detest pride, and cherish humility and truth, and never desert it, overcome either by flattery or by fear. Let him not put light for darkness, nor darkness for light: let him not call evil good, nor good evil. May he be a debtor to the wise and to the foolish, so that he may gather fruit from the progress of all. Grant to him, O Lord, an episcopal chair for ruling Thy Church and the people committed to him. Be his authority, be his power, be his strength. Multiply upon him Thy ✠ blessing and Thy grace, so that by Thy gift he may be

diam tuam tuo múnere idóneus et tua grátia possit esse devótus.

Deinde submissa voce dicit legendo, ita quod a circumstantibus audiri possit:

Per Dóminum nostrum Jesum Christum Fílium tuum: Qui tecum vivit, et regnat in unitáte Spíritus sancti Deus, per ómnia sǽcula sæculórum. ℟. Amen.

Post hæc Consecrator inchoat, schola prosequente, Antiphonam.

Ungéntum in cápite, quod descéndit in barbam, barbam Aaron, quod descéndit in oram vestiménti ejus: mandávit Dóminus benedictiónem in sæculum.

Psalmus 132.

ECCE quam bonum, et quam jucúndum: * habitáre fratres in unum.

Sicut unguéntum in cápite: * quod descéndit in barbam, barbam Aaron.

Quod descéndit in oram vestiménti ejus: * sicut ros Hermon, qui descéndit in montem Sion.

Quóniam illic mandávit Dóminus benedictiónem: * et vitam usque in sæculum.

Glória Patri, etc. Sicut erat in princípio, etc.

fitted for always obtaining Thy mercy, and by Thy grace may be faithful.

Then in a lower tone of voice he reads the following so as to be heard by those surrounding him:

Through Our Lord Jesus Christ, who liveth and reigneth in the unity of one God, world without end. R. Amen.

After this the Consecrator begins, and the choir takes up the Antiphon.

The ointment upon the head which descended on the beard, the beard of Aaron, which descended on the border of his vestment: the Lord hath commanded blessing forever.

Psalm 132.

BEHOLD how good and how pleasant it is for brethren to dwell together in unity:

Like the precious ointment on the head, that ran down upon the beard, the beard of Aaron.

Which ran down to the skirt of his garment: as the dew of Hermon, which descendeth upon mount Sion.

For there the Lord hath commanded blessing, and life for evermore.

Glory be to the Father, etc. As it was in the beginning, etc.

Deinde repetitur tota Antiphona, **Unguéntum in cápite,** etc.

Incepta Antiphona ante Psalmum, imponitur ad collum Electi alia ex longioribus mappulis, de octo supradictis. Consecrator sedet; accipit mitram; et Electo ante ipsum genuflexo inungit ambas manus simul junctas cum Chrismate in modum crucis, producendo cum pollice suo dextero intincto duas lineas; videlicet a pollice dexterae manus usque ad indicem sinistrae, et a pollice sinistrae usque ad indicem dexterae; et mox inungat totaliter palmas Electi, dicens:

UNGANTUR manus istæ de óleo sanctificáto, et Chrísmate sanctificatiónis, sicut unxit Sámuel David Regem, et Prophétam, ita ungántur, et consecréntur.

Et producens manu dextera ter signum crucis super manus Electi, dicit:

In nómine Dei Pa ✠ tris, et Fí ✠ lii, et Spíritus ✠ sancti, faciéntes imáginem sanctæ crucis Salvatóris nostri Jesu Christi, qui nos a morte redémit, et ad regna cœlórum perdúxit. Exaúdi nos, pie Pater omnípotens, ætérne Deus; et præsta, ut,

Then the whole Antiphon is repeated, **The ointment upon the head,** etc.

The Antiphon before the psalm having been begun, one of the longer strips from the eight above mentioned, is placed on the neck of the Bishop-elect. The Consecrator sits down, takes his mitre, whilst the Bishop-elect kneels before him, having his hands joined. Then the Consecrator anoints with chrism the hands of the Bishop-elect in the form of a cross, by drawing two lines with the thumb of his right hand, which has been dipped in the oil, namely, from the thumb of the right hand to the index finger of the left, and from the thumb of the left hand to the index finger of the right. And afterwards he anoints the entire palms of the Bishop-elect, saying:

MAY these hands be anointed with the sanctified oil and the chrism of sanctification, as Samuel anointed David to be King and Prophet; so may they be anointed and consecrated.

And making with his right hand the sign of the cross thrice over the hands of the Bishop-elect, he says:

In the name of God the ✠ Father, and of the ✠ Son, and of the Holy ✠ Ghost, making the image of the Holy cross of Our Saviour Jesus Christ, Who has redeemed us from death and led us to the kingdom of Heaven. Hear us, O loving, Almighty Father, Eternal God, and grant that we may obtain what we ask for.

quod te rogámus, exorémus. Per eúmdem Christum Dóminum nostrum.
R. Amen.

Et prosequitur sedens:

DEUS, et Pater Dómini nostri Jesu Christi, qui te ad Pontificátus sublimári vóluit dignitátem, ipse te Chrísmate, et mýsticæ delibutiónis liquóre perfúndat, et spirituális bene ✠ dictiónis ubertáte fœcúndet; quidquid bene ✠ díxeris, benedicátur; et quidquid sanctificáveris, sanctificétur; et consecrátæ manus istíus, vel póllicis impositio cunctis profíciat ad salútem.
R. Amen.

Præmissis itaque expeditis, Consecratus jungit ambas manus, et dexteram super sinistram tenet, et eas imponit mappulæ a collo dependenti. Consecrator vero abstergit paululum cum medulla panis pollicem; et, deposita mitra, surgit: et benedicit baculum Pastoralem, si non sit benedictus, dicens:

OREMUS.

SUSTENTATOR imbecillitátis humánæ Deus, béne ✠ dic báculum istum; et quod in eo extérius designátur, intérius in móribus hujus fámuli tui, tuæ

Through the same Christ Our Lord.
R. Amen.

Sitting down, he continues:

MAY God and the Father of Our Lord, Jesus Christ, Who hath Himself willed to elevate thee to the dignity of the Episcopate, bedew thee with chrism and with the liquor of mystic ointment, and make thee fruitful with the richness of spiritual ✠ benediction: Whatsoever you shall ✠ bless may it be blessed, and whatsoever you shall sanctify may it be sanctified; and may the imposition of this consecrated hand or thumb be profitable in all things unto salvation.
R. Amen.

After this, the one consecrated joins both hands, the right resting upon the left, and places them upon the cloth hanging from his neck. The Consecrator cleanses his thumb somewhat with some bread crumbs, and laying aside his mitre, rises and blesses the pastoral staff, if it has not been blessed, saying:

LET US PRAY.

O God, who dost sustain human weakness, bless ✠ this staff; and in the clemency of Thy merciful kindness, operate inwardly in the manners of this Thy

propitiatiónis cleméntia, operétur. Per Christum Dóminum nostrum.
℟. Amen.

Deinde illum aspergit aqua benedicta.

; · i sedens, accepta mitra, solus tradit illum Consecrato coram eo genuflexo, capienti ipsum inter indices, et medios digitos, manibus non disjunctis, Consecratore dicente:

ACCIPE báculum Pastorális offícii; ut sis in corrigéndis vítiis pie sǽviens, judícium sine ira tenens, in fovéndis virtútibus auditórum ánimos demúlcens, in tranquillitáte severitátis censúram non déserens.
℟. Amen.

Quo facto, deposita mitra, surgit Consecrator, et benedicit annulum, si non sit prius benedictus, dicens:

OREMUS.

CREATOR, et conservátor humáni géneris, dator grátiæ spirituális, largitor ætérnæ salútis, tu Dómine, emítte bene ✠ dictiónem tuam super hunc ánnulum; ut quicúmque hoc sacrosánctæ fídei signo insignítus incésserit, in virtúte cœléstis defensiónis ad ætérnam vitam sibi

servant, what it outwardly designates.
Through Christ Our Lord.
R. Amen.

Then he sprinkles it with holy water. Sitting down and taking his mitre, he himself hands the staff to the one consecrated, who is kneeling before him, and who receives it between the index and middle fingers, the hands remaining joined, while the Consecrator says:

RECEIVE the staff of the pastoral office, so that in the correction of vices you may be lovingly severe, giving judgment without wrath, softening the minds of your hearers whilst fostering virtues, not neglecting strictness of discipline through love of tranquillity.
R. Amen.

After which, laying aside the mitre, the Consecrator rises and blesses the ring, if it has not been blessed before, saying:

LET US PRAY.

O LORD, Creator and Preserver of the human race, Giver of spiritual grace, Bestower of eternal salvation, do Thou send forth Thy ✠ blessing upon this ring; so that whosoever shall be adorned with this sign of holiest fidelity, it may avail him by the power of heavenly pro-

profíciat.   Per Christum Dóminum nostrum.

℟. Amen.

Tum aspergit ipsum annulum aqua benedicta; sedet cum mitra et solus annulum in digitum annularem dexteræ manus Consecrati immittit, dicens:

ACCIPE ánnulum, fídei scílicet signáculum: quátenus sponsam Dei, sanctam vidélicet Ecclésiam, intemeráta fide ornátus, illibáte custódias.

℟. Amen.

Tum Consecrator accipit librum Evangeliorum de scapulis Consecrati; et, adjuvantibus ipsum Episcopis assistentibus, tradit eum clausum Consecrato, tangenti illum sine apertione manuum, dicens:

ACCIPE Evangélium, et vade, prædica pópulo tibi commísso; potens est enim Deus, ut aúgeat tibi grátiam suam: Qui vivit et regnat in sǽcula sæculórum.

℟. Amen.

tection unto eternal life. Through Christ
Our Lord.
　R. Amen.

He then sprinkles the ring with holy water, and sitting with his mitre on, himself places the ring on the ring finger of the right hand of the one consecrated, saying:

RECEIVE the ring, the symbol of fidelity, in order that, adorned with unspotted faith, you may keep inviolably the Spouse of God, namely, His Holy Church.
　R. Amen.

Then the Consecrator takes the book of the Gospels from the shoulders of the one consecrated, and with the aid of the assistant bishops, hands it closed to the one consecrated, the latter touching it without opening his hands, whilst the Consecrator says:

RECEIVE the Gospel and go preach to the people committed to thee, for God is powerful to increase his grace in thee, He who liveth and reigneth, world without end.
　R. Amen.

Finally the Consecrator receives the one consecrated to the kiss of peace. The assistant bishops each do likewise, saying to the one consecrated: **Peace be with thee.**

Et ipse respondet singulis: **Et cum spiritu tuo.**

Tum Consecratus medius inter assistentes Episcopos, redit ad capellam suam, ubi abstergitur ei sedenti caput cum medulla panis, et cum panno mundo; deinde cum pectine mundantur, et complanantur capilli; postea lavat manus. Consecrator vero in suo faldistorio manus lavat. Deinde procedit in Missa usque ad Offertorium inclusive. Idem facit Consecratus in capella sua.

Dicto Offertorio, Consecrator sedet cum mitra in faldistorio, ante medium altaris. Et Consecratus veniens ex sua capella, inter assistentes Episcopos medius coram Consecratore genuflectit; et illi offert duo intortitia accensa, duos panes, et duo barilia vino plena, et Consecratoris prædicta recipientis manum reverenter osculatur.

Deinde Consecrator lavat manus, et accedit ad altare; Consecratus etiam ad posterius cornu Epistolæ altaris ejusdem accedit: et ibi stans medius inter Episcopos assistentes ante se habens Missale suum, simul cum Consecratore dicit, et facit omnia, prout in Missali; et ponatur una Hostia consecranda pro Consecrante, et Consecrato, et vinum consecrandum, in Calice, sufficiens pro utroque.

Secreta sequens dicitur cum Secreta Missæ diei sub uno **Per Dóminum,** per Consecratorem.

And he answers to each: **And with thy spirit.**

Then the one consecrated, between the assistant **bishops**, returns to his chapel, where, while he is seated, his head is cleansed with some bread crumbs and with a clean cloth. Then his hair is cleansed, and combed; afterwards he washes his hands. The Consecrator washes his hands at his faldstool. Then he goes on with the Mass up to the Offertory inclusive. The consecrated does the same in his chapel.

The Offertory having been said, the Consecrator sits with his mitre on at the faldstool before the middle of the altar, and the one consecrated, coming from his chapel, between the assistant bishops, kneels before the Consecrator and offers to him two lighted torches, two loaves of bread and two small barrels of wine, and kisses reverently the hands of the Consecrator receiving the above gifts.

Then the Consecrator washes his hands and goes to the altar. The one consecrated also goes to the Epistle side of the same altar; there, standing between the assistant bishops, having before him his Missal, he says and does with the Consecrator everything as in the Missal. And one host is prepared to be consecrated for the Consecrator and the one consecrated, and wine sufficient for both is placed in the chalice.

The following Secret is said with the Secret of the Mass of the day under one **Through Our Lord** by the Consecrator.

SECRETA.

SUSCIPE, Dómine, múnera, quæ tibi offérimus pro hoc fámulo tuo; et propítius in eo tua dona custódias. Per Dóminum nostrum Jesum Christum Fílium tuum: Qui tecum vivit, et regnat in unitáte Spíritus sancti Deus, per ómnia sǽcula sæculórum.
℟. Amen.

Consecratus dicit:

SECRETA.

SUSCIPE, Dómine, múnera, quæ tibi offérimus pro me fámulo tuo; et propítius in me tua dona custódias. Per Dóminum nostrum Jesum Christum Fílium tuum: Qui tecum vivit, et regnat in unitáte Spíritus sancti Deus, per ómnia sǽcula sæculórum.
℟. Amen.

Infra actionem dicit Consecrator:

HANC ígitur oblatiónem servitútis nostræ, sed et cunctæ famíliæ tuæ, quam tibi offérimus, étiam pro hoc fámulo tuo, quem ad Episcopátus órdinem promovére dignátus es, quǽsumus Dómine, ut placátus accípias, et propítius in eo tua dona custódias; ut, quod divíno

SECRET.

RECEIVE, O Lord, the gifts which we offer to Thee for this Thy servant, and kindly preserve in him Thy favors. Through Our Lord Jesus Christ, Thy Son, who liveth and reigneth in the unity of the Holy Ghost, world without end.
R. Amen.

The one consecrated says:

SECRET.

RECEIVE, O Lord, the gifts which we offer to Thee for me, Thy servant, and kindly preserve Thy favors in me. Through Our Lord Jesus Christ, who liveth and reigneth in the unity of the Holy Ghost, world without end.
R. Amen.

During the action, the Consecrator says:

THIS oblation therefore, of our service, and that of Thy whole family which we offer Thee, also for this Thy servant, whom Thou hast vouchsafed to promote to the order of the episcopate, we beseech Thee, O Lord, graciously to accept, and to kindly preserve Thy favors in him, so that what has been accomplished by the

múnere consecútus est, divínis efféctibus exsequátur: diésque nostros in tua pace dispónas: atque ab ætérna damnatióne nos éripi, et in electórum tuórum júbeas grege numerári. Per Christum Dóminum nostrum.
℞ Amen.

Consecratus dicit:

HANC ígitur oblatiónem servitútis nostræ, sed et cunctæ famíliæ tuæ, quam tibi offérimus, étiam pro me fámulo tuo, quem ad Episcopátus órdinem promovére dignátus es, quæsumus Dómine, ut placátus accípias, et propítius in me tua dona custódias; ut, quod divíno múnere consecútus sum, divínis efféctibus éxsequar; diésque nostros in tua pace dispónas; atque ab ætérna damnatióne nos éripi, et in electórum tuórum júbeas grege numerári. Per Christum Dóminum nostrum.
R. Amen.

Dicta Oratione **Dómine Jesu Christe, qui,** etc., per Consecratorem et Consecratum, Consecratus accedit ad dexteram Consecratoris, et ambo osculantur altare; tum Consecrator dat pacem Consecrato, dicens: **Pax tecum.**

divine gift, may be followed by divine effects: and dispose our days in Thy peace, and command us to be delivered from eternal damnation, and to be numbered in the flock of Thine elect. Through Christ Our Lord.
℟. Amen.

The one consecrated says:

THIS oblation therefore, of our service, and that of Thy whole family which we offer Thee, also for me Thy servant, whom Thou hast vouchsafed to promote to the order of bishop, we beseech Thee, O Lord, graciously to accept and kindly to preserve in me Thy favors, so that what I have accomplished by the divine gift, I may complete by divine effects; and dispose our days in Thy peace, and command us to be delivered from eternal damnation and to be numbered in the flock of Thine elect. Through Christ Our Lord.
℟. Amen.

The prayer **Lord Jesus Christ, who,** etc., having been said by the Consecrator and the one consecrated, the latter goes up to the right of the Consecrator and both kiss the altar. Then the Consecrator gives the kiss of peace to the one consecrated saying: **Peace be with thee,** to whom the one consecrated answers: **And with thy**

33 DE CONSECRATIONE ELECTI IN EPISCOPUM.

Cui respondet Consecratus: **Et cum spíritu tuo.**
Et dat eam Assistentibus suis, seniori primo, tum alteri, singulis dicens: **Pax tibi.**
Et illi sibi respondent: **Et cum spíritu tuo.**

Deinde postquam Consecrator corpus Domini sumpserit, non totum sanguinem sumit, sed solum partem ejus cum particula Hostiæ in Calicem missa. Et priusquam se purificet, communicat Consecratum ante se in eodem cornu capite inclinato stantem, et non genuflectentem, prius de corpore, tum de sanguine, deinde purificat se, postea Consecratum. Tum abluit digitos super Calicem, et sumit etiam ablutionem; et, assumpta mitra, lavat manus.

Interim Consecratus cum assistentibus Episcopis accedit ad posteriorem partem alterius cornu altaris, videlicet Evangelii, et ibi prosequitur Missam, sicut Consecrator in cornu Epistolæ.

Postcommunio, quæ dici debet cum Postcommunione diei, sub uno **Per Dóminum.**

P LENUM, quæsumus Dómine, in nobis remédium tuæ miseratiónis operáre: ac tales nos esse pérfice propítius, et sic fove, ut tibi in ómnibus placére valeámus. Per Dóminum nostrum Jesum Christum

THE CONSECRATION OF A BISHOP.

spirit. and he gives the kiss of peace to his assistants, first to the senior, then to the other, saying to each: **Peace be with thee,** and they answer him: **And with thy spirit.**

Then after the Consecrator has consumed the Body of the Lord, he does not entirely consume the blood, but only a portion with the particle of the host that has been placed in the chalice, and before he takes the purification, he communicates the one consecrated, who stands with bowed head and not genuflecting, first giving him the Body and then the Blood. Then he purifies himself and afterwards the one consecrated. He then washes his fingers over the chalice and takes also the ablution, and having received the mitre, he washes his hands. Meanwhile, the one consecrated, with his assistant bishops, goes to the other corner of the altar, namely, the Gospel side, and there continues the Mass while the Consecrator does the same at the Epistle side.

The Post-Communion which ought to be said with the Post-Communion of the day under one **Through Our Lord Jesus Christ, Who liveth and reigneth.**

WE beseech Thee, O Lord, work in us the saving fulness of Thy mercy: and propitiously render us so perfect, and so cherish us that we may be able to please Thee in all things. Through Our Lord Jesus Christ, who with Thee liveth

34 DE CONSECRATIONE ELECTI IN EPISCOPUM

Fílium tuum : Qui tecum vivit, et regnat in unitáte Spíritus sancti Deus, per ómnia sǽcula sæculórum.
℟. Amen.

Deinde dicto, **Ite missa est,** vel **Benedicámus Dómino,** prout tempus requirit, Consecrato dicto in medio altaris, **Pláceat,** etc.. accepta ibidem mitra, si non sit Archiepiscopus, et in sua provincia, stans versus ad altare, populo solemniter benedicit, dicens: **Sit nomen Dómini benedíctum,** etc.

Data benedictione, reponitur faldistorium ante medium altaris, et Consecrator cum mitra in eo sedet: Consecratus vero parvum biretum in capite tenens coram eo genuflectit. Tum Consecrator, deposita mitra, surgit, et benedicit mitram, si non sit benedicta, dicens:

OREMUS.

DOMINE Deus, Pater omnípotens, cujus præclára bónitas est, et virtus imménsa, a qua omne datum óptimum, et omne donum perféctum, totiúsque decóris ornaméntum, bene ✠ dícere, et sanctí ✠ ficáre dignáre hanc mitram hujus fámuli tui Antístitis cápiti imponéndam. Per Christum Dóminum nostrum.
℟. Amen.

and reigneth in the unity of the Holy Ghost, world without end.
R. Amen.

Then after **Go, Mass is ended,** or **Let us bless the Lord,** as the time requires, has been said, the Consecrator having said **May the performance,** etc., in the middle of the altar, and received there the mitre, if he be not an Archbishop, and in his province, turned towards the altar, he solemnly blesses the people, saying: **Blessed be the name of the Lord,** etc.

Having given the Benediction, the Consecrator, with his mitre on, sits on the faldstool which has been placed before the middle of the altar: the one consecrated, keeping his biretta on his head, kneels before him. Then the Consecrator, having laid aside his mitre, rises and blesses the mitre, if it has not been blessed, saying:

LET US PRAY.

O Lord God, Father Almighty, whose goodness is wonderful and whose power immense, from whom is every best and every perfect gift, the ornament of all beauty, vouchsafe to ✠ bless and ✠ sanctify this mitre to be placed on the head of this Prelate Thy servant. Through Christ Our Lord.
R. Amen.

Et mox eam aspergit aqua benedicta; deinde sedens cum mitra, adjuvantibus ipsum assistentibus Episcopis, imponit eam capiti Consecrati, dicens:

IMPONIMUS, Dómine, cápiti hujus Antístitis et agonístæ tui gáleam munitiónis et salútis, quátenus decoráta fácie, et armáto cápite, córnibus utriúsque Testaménti terríbilis appáreat adversáriis veritátis; et, te ei largiénte grátiam, impugnátor eórum robústus exsístat, qui Móysi fámuli tui fáciem ex tui sermónis consórtio decorátam, lucidíssimis tuæ claritátis ac veritátis córnibus insignísti; et cápiti Aaron Pontíficis tui tiáram impóni jussísti. Per Christum Dóminum nostrum.
R. Amen.

Deinde, si chirothecæ non sint benedictæ, surgit Consecrator, mitra deposita, et eas benedicit, dicens:

OREMUS.

OMNIPOTENS Creátor, qui hómini ad imáginem tuam cóndito manus discretiónis insignítas, tamquam órganum intelligéntiæ, ad recte operándum dedísti:

And then he sprinkles it with holy water, after which, sitting down with his mitre on, the assistant bishops aiding him, he places it on the head of the one consecrated, saying:

WE, O Lord, place on the head of this Thy bishop and champion, the helmet of protection and salvation, so that his face being adorned and his head armed with the horns of both testaments, he may seem terrible to the opponents of truth, and through the indulgence of Thy grace may be their sturdy adversary, Thou Who didst mark with the brightest rays of Thy splendor and truth the countenance of Moses Thy servant, ornamented from his fellowship with Thy word : and didst order the tiara to be placed on the head of Aaron thy high priest. Through Christ Our Lord.
R. Amen.

Then if the gloves have not been blessed, the Consecrator rises, having laid aside the mitre, and blesses them, saying:

LET US PRAY.

O Almighty Creator, Who hast given to man fashioned after Thy image, hands notable for their formation, as an organ of intelligence for correct workmanship:

quas servári mundas præcepísti, ut in eis ánima digne portarétur, et tua in eis digne consecraréntur mystéria, bene ✠ dícere, et sancti ✠ficáre dignáre mánuum hæc teguménta; ut quicúmque ministrórum tuórum sacrórum Pontíficum his veláre manus suas cum humilitáte volúerit, tam cordis, quam óperis ei mundítiam tua misericórdia submiínistret. Per Christum Dóminum nostrum.
R. Amen.

Et aspergit eas aqua benedicta. Tunc extrahitur Consecrato annulus Pontificalis; deinde sedet Consecrator, et accepta mitra, adjuvantibus assistentibus Episcopis, imponit illas manibus Consecrati, dicens:

CIRCUMDA, Dómine, manus hujus minístri tui mundítia novi hóminis, qui de cœlo descéndit, ut quemádmodum Jacob diléctus tuus, pellículis hædórum opértis mánibus, patérnam benedictiónem, obláto patri cibo, potúque gratissimo, impetrávit, sic et iste, obláta per manus suas hóstia salutári, grátiæ tuæ benedictiónem impetráre mereátur. Per Dóminum nostrum Jesum Christum Fílium tuum; qui

which Thou hast commanded to be kept clean, so that the soul might worthily be carried in them and Thy mysteries worthily consecrated by them, vouchsafe to ✠ bless and ✠ sanctify these hand coverings, so that whosoever of Thy ministers, the holy Bishops, shall humbly wish to cover their hands with these, Thy mercy shall accord to him cleanness of heart as well as of deed. Through Christ Our Lord.

R. Amen.

And he sprinkles them with holy water. Then the pontifical ring is drawn from the finger of the one consecrated, the Consecrator sits down and having received the mitre with the aid of the assistant bishops, places the gloves on the hands of the one consecrated, saying:

ENCOMPASS, O Lord, the hands of this Thy minister with the cleanness of the new man who descended from Heaven, so that as Thy beloved Jacob, his hands covered with the skins of young goats, implored and received the paternal benediction, having offered to his Father most agreeable food and drink, so also this one may deserve to implore and to receive the benediction of Thy grace by means of the saving host offered by his hands. Through Our Lord Jesus Christ,

DE CONSECRATIONE ELECTI IN EPISCOPUM.

in similitúdinem carnis peccáti tibi pro nobis óbtulit semetípsum.
R. Amen.

Et statim imponit ei annulum Pontificalem. Tum surgit Consecrator, et accipit Consecratum per manum dexteram, et primus ex assistentibus Episcopis per sinistram, et inthronizat eum, ponendo ipsum ad sedendum in faldistorio, de quo surrexit Consecrator, vel, si id fiat in Ecclesia propria Consecrati, inthronizant eum in sede Episcopali consueta; et Consecrator tradit ei baculum Pastoralem in sinistra.

Deinde versus ad altare Consecrator, deposita mitra, stans incipit, cæteris usque ad finem prosequentibus Hymnum: **Te Deum Laudamus**, prout in Appendice. p. 9*.

Incepto Hymno, Consecratus ducitur ab assistentibus Episcopis cum mitris per Ecclesiam; et omnibus benedicit, Consecratore interim apud altare sine mitra stante in eodem loco. Cum vero Consecratus reversus fuerit ad sedem suam, seu faldistorium, iterum sedet, quousque finiatur Hymnus prædictus; Assistentes deponunt mitras, et stant apud Consecratorem.

Finito Hymno, Consecrator stans sine mitra apud sedem, seu faldistorium a parte dextera Consecrati dicit; vel si Officium cantatur, incipit, schola prosequente, Antiphonam :

Thy Son, who in the likeness of sinful flesh, offered himself to Thee for us.

And immediately he places on the finger of the one consecrated the Episcopal ring. Then the Consecrator rises and takes the one consecrated by the right hand, and the senior assistant bishop takes him by the left, and they enthrone him by placing him sitting on the faldstool from which the Consecrator has risen, or if the ceremony be performed in the Church of the one consecrated, they enthrone him on the usual episcopal seat, and the Consecrator places in his left hand the pastoral staff.

Then the Consecrator, turning towards the altar and laying aside the mitre, while standing, begins, the others taking it up and finishing it, the Hymn. **We praise Thee O Lord.***

At the beginning of the hymn, the one consecrated is led by the assistant bishops with their mitres on around the Church, and he blesses everyone. The Consecrator meanwhile without his mitre remains standing in the same place at the altar. When the one consecrated has returned to his seat or the faldstool, he sits again until the above mentioned hymn is finished. The assistants lay aside their mitres and stand with the Consecrator.

At the conclusion of the hymn, the Consecrator, standing without his mitre, at the throne, or the faldstool at the right hand of the one consecrated, says; or if the office be sung, he begins, the choir taking up the Antiphon.

---

* See Appendix. p. 9*.

38 DE CONSECRATIONE ELECTI IN EPISCOPUM.

Firmétur manus tua, et exaltétur déxtera tua: justítia et judícium præparátio sedis tuæ. Glória Patri, et Fílio, et Spirítui sancto. Sicut erat in princípio, et nunc, et semper, et in sǽcula sæculórum. Amen.

Et repetitur tota Antiphona; qua finita, Consecrator dicit:

℣. Dómine exaúdi oratiónem meam.
℟. Et clamor meus ad te véniat.
℣. Dóminus vobíscum.
℟. Et cum spíritu tuo.

OREMUS.

DEUS, ómnium fidélium pastor, et rector, hunc fámulum tuum, quem Ecclésiæ tuæ præésse voluísti, propítius réspice: da ei, quǽsumus, verbo et exémplo, quibus præest profícere; ut ad vitam, una cum grege sibi crédito, pervéniat sempitérnam. Per Christum Dóminum nostrum.
℟. Amen.

His dictis, Consecrator, detecto capite, manet ad cornu Evangelii altaris, apud quem Assistentes stant sine mitris.

May Thy hand be strengthened and Thy right hand be exalted, justice and judgment be the preparation of Thy throne. Glory be to the Father, and to the Son, and to the Holy Ghost, as it was in the beginning, is now and ever shall be, world without end.

And the whole Antiphon is repeated. When this is finished the Consecrator says:

V. O Lord, hear my prayer.
R. And let my cry come unto Thee.
V. The Lord be with you.
R. And with thy spirit.

LET US PRAY.

O GOD, the Pastor and Ruler of all the faithful, look down in Thy mercy upon this Thy servant, whom Thou hast appointed over Thy Church, and grant, we beseech Thee, that both by word and example, he may edify all those who are under his charge, so that with the flock intrusted to him, he may attain unto life everlasting. Through Christ Our Lord.
R. Amen.

After which the Consecrator, with uncovered head, remains at the Gospel corner of the altar, the assistants, also uncovered, standing with him.

39 DE CONSECRATIONE ELECTI IN EPISCOPUM.

Consecratus vero surgit, et accedens cum mitra, et baculo Pastorali ante medium altaris, versus ad illud, signans se cum pollice dexteræ manus ante pectus, dicit:

Sit nomen Dómini benedíctum.
R. **Ex hoc nunc et usque in sǽculum.**

Deinde faciens signum crucis a fronte ad pectus, dicit:

Adjutórium nostrum in nómine Dómini.
R. **Qui fecit coelum et terram.**

Tum elevans, ac jungens manus, et caput inclinans, dicit:

Benedícat vos omnípotens Deus.

Et cum dixerit **Deus**, vertit se ad populum et tertio super eum signans benedicit, dicens:

Pa✠ ter, et Fí✠ lius, et Spíritus✠ sanctus.
R. Amen.

Tum Consecrator accipit mitram, stans in cornu Evangelii, versa facie ad cornu Epistolæ: apud quem etiam stant Assistentes cum mitris; Consecratus vero accedit ad cornu Epistolæ altaris; et ibidem cum mitra, et baculo genuflexus versus ad Consecratorem, dicit cantando:

Ad multos annos.

Deinde accedens ante medium altaris, ubi iterum, ut prius genuflexus, dicit altius cantando:

The one consecrated rises, and going with his mitre and his pastoral staff before the middle of the altar, turns towards it; and, signing himself with the thumb of his right hand before his breast, he says:

Blessed be the name of the Lord.

R. Now and forever.

Then making the sign of the cross from his forehead to his breast, the says:

Our help is in the name of the Lord.

R. Who hath made Heaven and earth.

Then raising and joining his hands, and bowing his head, he says:

May the Almighty God bless you.

And when he has said " **God** " he turns towards the people and blesses them thrice, saying:

The ✠Father, the ✠Son and the Holy ✠Ghost.

R. Amen.

Then the Consecrator takes his mitre, and stands at the Gospel corner, his face turned towards the Epistle corner. The assistants, with their mitres on, stand near him. The one consecrated goes to the epistle corner of the altar, and there with his mitre on, and holding his staff, facing the Consecrator, he makes a genuflection and sings:

For many years.

Then going to the middle of the altar, he again genuflects as before, and says, singing in a higher voice:

Ad multos annos :

Postea accedit ad pedes Consecratoris, ubi tertio genuflexus, ut supra, iterum altius cantando dicit:

Ad multos annos.

Tum Consecrator recipit eum surgentem ad osculum pacis; et similiter faciunt assistentes Episcopi, qui Consecratum cum mitra, et baculo Pastorali incedentem, et Evangelium sancti Joannis, **In princípio erat Verbum,** etc. dicentem, post reverentiam cruci super altare factam, inter se medium ducentes, ad suam capellam revertuntur, ad se exuendum sacris vestibus, et interim dicit Antiphonam. **Trium puerórum,** et Canticum. **Benedícite,** etc. Consecrator vero, pacis osculo, ut præmittitur, Consecrato dato, dicit submissa voce: **Dóminus vobíscum.**

Inítium sancti Evangélii secúndum Joánnem.

In princípio erat Verbum, etc.

Signat altare, et se; et facta similiter cruci reverentia, apud sedem vel faldistorium deponit sacras vestes, interim etiam dicens Antiphonam. **Trium puerórum,** et Canticum. **Benedícite,** etc. quibus depositis, Consecratus Consecratori, et Assistentibus suis pro more gratias agit; et vadunt in pace omnes.

THE CONSECRATION OF A BISHOP.

For many years.

Afterwards he goes to the feet of the Consecrator and genuflecting a third time as above, he sings again in a still higher tone of voice:
For many years.

Then when he has risen the Consecrator receives him to the kiss of peace. The assistant bishops do likewise. These lead between them the one consecrated, who wears his mitre and walks with the pastoral staff, reciting the Gospel of St. John, **In the beginning was the Word,** etc. After having made a reverence to the cross upon the altar he goes to his chapel, where he lays aside his vestments saying meanwhile the antiphon **Of the Three children,** etc., and the canticle, **'Bless ye.'** The Consecrator, having given the kiss of peace to the one consecrated, says in a low voice: **The Lord be with you, The beginning of the Gospel according to St. John. In the beginning was the Word,** etc. He signs the altar and himself, and having made likewise a reverence to the cross, he lays aside his sacred vestments at the throne or the faldstool, saying also the antiphon **Of the three children** and the canticle **'Bless ye,'** etc., after which the one consecrated returns thanks to the Consecrator and his assistants, and all depart in peace.

APPENDIX.

Per natalitium Apostolorum intelligitur stricte dies qua migravit Sanctus in cœlum: itaque consecratio fieri non potest sine indulto in Festo Conversionis Sancti Pauli. In Liturgia Evangelista æquiparatur Apostolo: consecratio igitur fieri potest in Festis Evangelistarum. Ita De Herdt, t ii, n. 272 ad 3um; Gavantus, Com. in Rub. Miss. Rom. t iii. Sec. viii. cap. ii. n° 1 et Nota, no. 1.

Litaniæ Sanctorum.

Kyrie eléison.
Christe eléison.
Kyrie eléison.
Christe audi nos.
Christe exaudi nos.
Pater de cœlis Deus,
Fili Redémptor mundi Deus,
Spíritus Sancte Deus,
Sancta Trínitas, unus Deus, } *Miserere nobis.*
Sancta María, *ora pro nobis.*
Sancta Dei Génitrix, *ora pro nobis.*
Sancta Vírgo vírginum,
Sancte Míchaël,
Sancte Gábriel,
Sancte Ráphaël, } *Ora pro nobis.*
Omnes sáncti Angeli, et Archángeli, *oráte pro nobis.*
Omnes sancti beatórum Spirítuum órdines, *oráte pro nobis.*

APPENDIX.

By *natalitium Apostolorum* is meant the feast day commemorating the death of an Apostle. It is not permitted, therefore, to have the consecration without an Indult on such a day as The Feast of the Conversion of St. Paul. In Liturgy an Evangelist is regarded as an Apostle; the consecration therefore can take place on the Feast of an Evangelist. See De Herdt, vol. 2. n. 272, note 3; Gavantus, Com. in Rub. Miss. vol. 3. sec. 8, chap. 2. n. 1 and Note no. 1.

The Litany of the Saints.

Lord, have mercy on us.
Christ, have mercy on us.
Lord, have mercy on us.
Christ, hear us.
Christ, graciously hear us.
God the Father of heaven,
God the Son, Redeemer of the world, } *Have mercy on us.*
God the Holy Ghost,
Holy Trinity, one God,
Holy Mary, *pray for us.*
Holy Mother of God, *pray for us.*
Holy Virgin of virgins,
St. Michael,
St. Gabriel, } *Pray for us.*
St. Raphael,
All ye holy Angels and Archangels,
All ye holy orders of blessed Spirits,

Sancte Joánnes Baptísta, *ora pro nobis.*
Sancte Joseph, *ora pro nobis.*
Omnes sancti Patriárchæ, et Prophétæ, *oráte.*
Sancte Petre,
Sancte Paule,
Sancte Andréa,
Sancte Jacóbe,
Sancte Joánnes,
Sancte Thoma,
Sancte Jacóbe,
Sancte Philíppe,
Sancte Bartholomǽe,
Sancte Matthǽe,
Sancte Simon,
Sancte Thaddǽe,
Sancte Mathía,
Sancte Bárnaba,
Sancte Luca,
Sancte Marce,
Omnes sancti Apóstoli, et Evangelístæ,
Omnes sancti Discípuli Dómini,
Omnes sancti Innocéntes,
Sancte Stéphane,
Sancte Lauŕenti,
Sancte Vincénti,
Sancti Fabiáne et Sebastiáne,
Sancti Joánnes et Paule,
Sancti Cosma et Damiáne,
Sancti Gervási et Protási,
Omnes sancti Mártyres,

St. John the Baptist,
St. Joseph,
All ye holy Patriarchs and Prophets,
St. Peter,
St. Paul,
St. Andrew,
St. James,
St. John,
St. Thomas,
St. James,
St. Philip,
St. Bartholomew,
St. Matthew,
St. Simon,
St. Thaddeus,
St. Matthias,
St. Barnabas,
St. Luke,
St. Mark,
All ye holy Apostles and Evangelists,
All ye holy Disciples of the Lord,
All ye holy Innocents,
St. Stephen,
St. Lawrence,
St. Vincent,
SS. Fabian and Sebastian,
SS. John and Paul,
SS. Cosmas and Damian,
SS Gervase and Protase,
All ye holy Martyrs,

Pray for us.

Sancte Silvéster,
Sancte Gregóri,
Sancte Ambrósi,
Sancte Augustíne,
Sancte Hierónyme,
Sancte Martíne,
Sancte Nicoláe, } *Ora, etc.*
Omnes sancti Pontífices, et Confessóres,
   oráte pro nobis.
Omnes sancti Doctóres, *oráte pro nobis.*
Sancte Antóni,
Sancte Benedícte,
Sancte Bernárde,
Sancte Domínice,
Sancte Francísce, } *Ora pro nobis.*
Omnes sancti Sacerdótes, et Levítæ,
   oráte pro nobis.
Omnes sancti Mónachi, et Eremítæ,
   oráte pro nobis.
Sancta María Magdaléna,
Sancta Agatha,
Sancta Lúcia,
Sancta Agnes,
Sancta Cæcília,
Sancta Catharína,
Sancta Anastásia, } *Ora pro nobis.*
Omnes sanctæ Vírgines et Víduæ,
   oráte pro nobis.
Omnes Sancti et Sanctæ Dei,
   intercédite pro nobis.

LITANY OF THE SAINTS.

St. Sylvester,
St. Gregory,
St. Ambrose,
St. Augustine,
St. Jerome,
St. Martin,
St. Nicholas,
All ye holy Bishops and Confessors,
All ye holy Doctors,
St. Anthony,
St. Benedict,
St. Bernard,
St. Dominic,
St. Francis,
All ye holy Priests and Levites,
All ye holy Monks and Hermits,
St. Mary Magdalen,
St. Agatha,
St. Lucy,
St. Agnes,
St. Cecilia,
St. Catherine,
St. Anastasia,
All ye holy Virgins and Widows,
All ye holy Saints of God,
  Make intercession for us.

Pray for us.

Propítius esto, *parce nobis Dómine.*
Propítius esto, *exaúdi nos Dómine.*
Ab omni malo, *líbera nos Dómine.*
Ab omni peccáto, *líbera nos Dómine.*
Ab ira tua,
A subitánea et improvísa morte,
Ab insídiis diáboli,
Ab ira, et ódio, et omni mala voluntáte,
A spíritu fornicatiónis,
A fúlgure et tempestáte,
A flagéllo terræmótus,
A peste, fame, et bello,
A morte perpétua,
Per mystérium sanctæ incarnatiónis tuæ,
Per advéntum tuum,
Per nativitátem tuam,
Per baptísmum et sanctum jejúnium tuum,
Per crúcem et passiónem tuam,
Per mortem et sepultúram tuam,
Per sanctam resurrectiónem tuam,
Per admirábilem ascensiónem tuam,
Per advéntum Spíritus sancti Parácliti,
In die judícii,
Peccatóres, *te rogámus audi nos,*

Líbera nos Dómine.

LITANY OF THE SAINTS.

Be merciful,
Spare us, O Lord.
Be merciful,
Graciously hear us, O Lord.
From all evil, *O Lord, deliver us.*
From all sin, *O Lord, deliver us.*
From Thy wrath,
From sudden and unlooked-for death,
From the snares of the devil,
From anger, and hatred, and every evil will,
From the spirit of fornication,
From lightning and tempest,
From the scourge of earthquakes,
From plague, famine and war,
From everlasting death,
Through the mystery of Thy holy Incarnation,
Through Thy Coming,
Through Thy Birth,
Through Thy Baptism and holy Fasting,
Through Thy Cross and Passion,
Through Thy Death and Burial,
Through Thy holy Resurrection,
Through Thine admirable Ascension,
Through the coming of the Holy Ghost, the Paraclete.
In the day of judgment. } *O Lord, deliver us.*
We sinners, *Beseech Thee, hear us.*

Ut nobis parcas,
Ut nobis indúlgeas,
Ut ad veram pœniténtiam nos perdúcere dignéris,
Ut Ecclésiam tuam sanctam régere, et conserváre dignéris,
Ut Domnum apostólicum, et omnes ecclesiásticos órdines in sancta religióne conserváre dignéris,
Ut inimícos sanctæ Ecclésiæ humiliáre dignéris,
Ut Régibus et Princípibus christiánis pacem et veram concórdiam donáre dignéris,
Ut cuncto pópulo christiáno pacem et unitátem largíri dignéris,
Ut nosmetípsos in tuo sancto servítio confortáre, et conserváre dignéris,
Ut mentes nostras ad cœléstia desidéria érigas,
Ut ómnibus benefactóribus nostris sempitérna bona retríbuas,
Ut ánimas nostras, fratrum, propinquórum, et benefactórum nostrórum ab ætérna damnatióne erípias,

Te rogámus audi nos.

That Thou wouldst spare us,
That Thou wouldst pardon us,
That Thou wouldst bring us to true penance,
That Thou wouldst vouchsafe to govern and preserve Thy holy Church,
That Thou wouldst vouchsafe to preserve our Apostolic Prelate, and all orders of the Church in holy religion,
That Thou wouldst vouchsafe to humble the enemies of holy Church,
That Thou wouldst vouchsafe to give peace and true concord to Christian kings and princes,
That Thou wouldst vouchsafe to grant peace and unity to the whole Christian world,
That Thou wouldst vouchsafe to confirm and preserve us in Thy holy service,
That Thou wouldst lift up our minds to heavenly desires,
That Thou wouldst render eternal blessings to all our benefactors,
That Thou wouldst deliver our souls, and the souls of our brethren, relations, and benefactors, from eternal damnation,

We beseech Thee, hear us.

Ut fructus terræ dare et conserváre dignéris.
Ut ómnibus fidélibus defúnctis réquiem ætérnam donáre dignéris.

} *Te rogámus, audi nos.*

Ut nos exaudíre dignéris, *te rogámus audi nos.*
Fili Dei, *te rogámus audi nos.*
Agnus Dei, qui tollis peccáta mundi, *Parce nobis Dómine.*

That Thou wouldst vouchsafe to give and preserve the fruits of the earth,
That Thou wouldst vouchsafe to grant eternal rest to all the faithful departed, *We beseech Thee, hear us.*
That Thou wouldst vouchsafe graciously to hear us, *we beseech Thee, hear us.*
Son of God, *we beseech Thee, hear us.*
Lamb of God, who takest away the sins of the world, *spare us, O Lord.*

VENI CREATOR.

Veni Creátor Spíritus,
Mentes tuórum vísita,
Imple supérna grátia,
Quæ tu creásti, péctora.

Qui díceris Paráclitus,
Altíssimi donum Dei,
Fons vivus, ignis, cáritas,
Et spiritális únctio.

Tu septifórmis múnere,
Dígitus Patérnæ déxteræ,
Tu rite promíssum Patris,
Sermóne ditans gúttura.

Accénde lumen sénsibus,
Infúnde amórem córdibus,
Infirma nostri córporis
Virtúte firmans pérpeti.

VENI CREATOR.

Come, Holy Ghost, Creator, come,
    From thy bright heavenly throne!
Come, take possession of our souls,
    And make them all Thine Own!

Thou who art called the Paraclete,
    Best gift of God above,
The Living Spring, the Living Fire,
    Sweet Unction, and True Love!

Thou who art sevenfold in Thy grace,
    Finger of God's right hand,
His Promise, teaching little ones
    To speak and understand!

O guide our minds with thy blest light,
    With love our hearts inflame,
And with thy strength, which ne'er
    Confirm our mortal frame.   [decays,

Hostem repéllas lóngius,
Pacémque dones prótinus;
Ductóresic te præ̀vio,
Vitémus omne nóxium.

Per te sciámus da Patrem
Noscámus atque Fílium ;
Teque utrius que Spíritum
Credámus omni témpore.

Deo Patri sit glória,
Et Filio, qui a mórtuis
Surréxit, ac Paráclito
In sacculórum sæcula.
   R. Amen.

Far from us drive our hellish foe,
   True peace unto us bring,
And through all perils guide us safe
   Beneath thy sacred wing.

Through Thee may we the Father know,
   Through Thee the Eternal Son,
And Thee the Spirit of them both—
   Thrice blessed Three in One.

Now to the Father, and the Son
   Who rose from death, be glory given,
With Thee, O holy Comforter,
   Henceforth by all in earth and heaven.
   R. Amen.

TE DEUM LAUDAMUS.

Te Deum laudamus:
Te Dóminum confitémur.
Te ætérnum Patrem * omnis terra venerátur.
Tibi omnes Angeli, * tibi cœli et univérsæ potestátes.
Tibi Chérubim et Séraphim * incessábili voce proclámant:
Sanctus, Sanctus, Sanctus * Dóminus Deus Sábaoth.
Pleni sunt cœli et terra * majestátis glóriæ tuæ.
Te gloriósus * Apostolórum chorus,
Te Prophetárum * laudábilis númerus,
Te Mártyrum candidátus * laudat exércitus.
Te per obem terrárum * sancta confitétur Ecclésia.
Patrem * imménsæ majestátis.
Venerándum tuum verum * et únicum Fílium,
Sanctum quoque * Paráclitum Spíritum.
Tu Rex glóriæ * Christe.
Tu Patris * sempitérnus es Fílius.

TE DEUM LAUDAMUS.

We praise Thee, O God : * we acknowledge Thee to be the Lord.
All the earth doth worship Thee * and the Father everlasting.
To Thee all Angels : * to Thee the Heavens and all the Powers therein.
To Thee the Cherubim and Seraphim : * cry with unceasing voice :
Holy, Holy, Holy : * Lord God of Hosts.
The heavens and the earth are full : * of the majesty of Thy glory.
Thee the glorious choir : * of the Apostles.
Thee the admirable company : * of the Prophets.
Thee the white-robed army of Martyrs : * praise.
Thee the Holy Church throughout all the world : * doth acknowledge.
The Father * of infinite Majesty.
Thine adorable, true : * and only Son.
Also the Holy Ghost : * the Paraclete.
Thou art the King of Glory : * O Christ.
Thou art the everlasting Son : * of the Father.

Tu ad liberándum susceptúrus hóminem,*
non horruísti Virginis úterum.
Tu, devícto mortis acúleo, * aperuísti
credéntibus regna cœlórum.
Tu ad déxteram Dei sedes * in glória Patris.
Judex créderis * esse ventúrus.
Te ergo quǽsumus, tuis fámulis súbveni,*
quos pretióso sánguine redemísti.
Ætérna fac cum Sanctis tuis * in glória
numerári.
Salvum fac pópulum tuum, Dómine : * et
bénedic hæreditáti tuæ.
Et rege eos, * et extólle illos usque in
ætérnum.
Per síngulos dies * benedícimus te.
Et laudámus nomen tuum in sǽculum, *
et in sǽculum sǽculi.
Dignáre, Dómine die isto * sine peccáto
nos custodíre.
Miserére nostri Dómine, * miserére nostri.
Fiat misercórdia tua Dómine super nos ; *
quemádmodum sperávimus in te.
In te Dómine sperávi ; * non confúndar
in ætérnum.

Thou having taken upon Thee to deliver man : * didst not abhor the Virgin's womb.
Thou having overcome the sting of death :* didst open to believers the kingdom of heaven.
Thou sittest at the right hand of God : * in the glory of the Father.
We believe that Thou shalt come : * to be our Judge.
We beseech Thee, therefore, help Thy servants : * whom Thou hast redeemed with Thy precious Blood.
Make them to be numbered with Thy Saints : * in glory everlasting.
O Lord, save Thy people : * and bless Thine inheritance.
Govern them : * and lift them up forever.
Day by day : * we bless Thee.
And we praise Thy name forever : * and world without end.
Vouchsafe, O Lord, this day : * to keep us without sin.
Have mercy on us, O Lord : * have mercy on us.
Let Thy mercy, O Lord, be upon us : * as we have hoped in Thee.
O Lord, in Thee have I hoped : * let me never be confounded.

www.ingramcontent.com/pod-product-compliance
Lightning Source LLC
Chambersburg PA
CBHW031409160426
43196CB00007B/956